![STANLEY] COMPLETE

DOORS
& WINDOWS

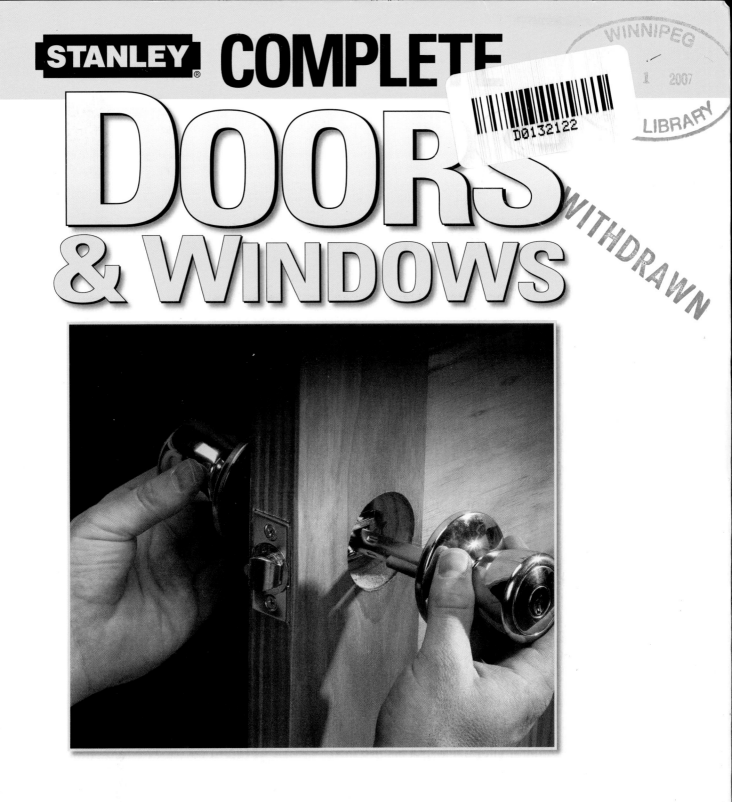

Meredith® **Books**
Des Moines, Iowa

Stanley Complete Doors & Windows
Editor: Larry Johnston
Copy Chief: Terri Fredrickson
Publishing Operations Manager: Karen Schirm
Senior Editor, Asset and Information Manager: Phillip Morgan
Edit and Design Production Coordinator: Mary Lee Gavin
Editorial and Design Assistant: Renee E. McAtee
Book Production Managers: Pam Kvitne,
    Marjorie J. Schenkelberg, Rick von Holdt, Mark Weaver
Contributing Copy Editor: Susan Fagen
Contributing Proofreaders: David Craft, Beth Lastine,
    Cheri Madison
Indexer: Don Glassman

**Additonal Editorial Contributions from
    Greenleaf Publishing**
Publishing Director: Dave Toht
Writer: Steve Cory
Editorial Art Director: Jean DeVaty
Design: Rebecca Anderson
Editorial Assistant: Betony Toht
Photography: Dan Stultz, Stultz Photography
Technical Consultant: Joe Hansa
Indexer: Nan Badgett

**Additional Editoral Contributions from
    Art Rep Services**
Director: Chip Nadeau
Illustrator: Dave Brandon

Meredith® Books
Executive Director, Editorial: Gregory H. Kayko
Executive Director, Design: Matt Strelecki
Managing Editor: Amy Tincher-Durik
Executive Editor/Group Manager: Benjamin Allen
Senior Associate Design Director: Tom Wegner
Marketing Product Manager: Brent Wiersma

Publisher and Editor in Chief: James D. Blume
Editorial Director: Linda Raglan Cunningham
Executive Director, New Business Development: Todd M. Davis
Executive Director, Sales: Ken Zagor
Director, Operations: George A. Susral
Director, Production: Douglas M. Johnston
Director, Marketing: Amy Nichols
Business Director: Jim Leonard

Vice President and General Manager: Douglas J. Guendel

Meredith Publishing Group
President: Jack Griffin
Executive Vice President: Karla Jeffries

Meredith Corporation
Chairman of the Board: William T. Kerr
President and Chief Executive Officer: Stephen M. Lacy

In Memoriam: E. T. Meredith III (1933–2003)

Special thanks to:
Andersen Corp.; JELD-WEN , Inc.; Milgard Windows, Inc.;
Pella Corp.; Pittsburgh Corning Corp.; Windo-Therm

All of us at Meredith® Books are dedicated to providing you
with the information and ideas you need to enhance your home
and garden. We welcome your comments and suggestions
about this book. Write to us at:
    Meredith Corporation
    Meredith Books
    1716 Locust St.
    Des Moines, IA 50309-3203

If you would like more information on other Stanley products,
call 1-800-STANLEY or visit us at: www.stanleyworks.com
Stanley® and the notched rectangle around the Stanley
name are registered trademarks of The Stanley Works and
subsidiaries.

Note to the Readers: Due to differing conditions, tools, and
individual skills, Meredith Corporation assumes no responsibility
for any damages, injuries suffered, or losses incurred as a
result of following the information published in this book.
Before beginning any project, review the instructions carefully,
and if any doubts or questions remain, consult local experts
or authorities. Because codes and regulations vary greatly,
you always should check with authorities to ensure that your
project complies with all applicable local codes and regulations.
Always read and observe all of the safety precautions provided
by manufacturers of any tools, equipment, or supplies, and
follow all accepted safety procedures.

CONTENTS

REFERENCE CHARTS

GLUES FOR CARPENTRY

TYPE	PROPERTIES
Aliphatic resin	Yellow glue. Strong, grabs fast. Moisture resistant, not waterproof. Corrodes steel. Popular wood glue.
Construction adhesive	Often sold in caulking-gun tubes. Thick, strong. Formulations for many construction purposes.
Cyanoacrylate ester	Bonds instantly to many materials (including skin). Strong, not shock resistant. Requires tight joint.
Epoxy	Strong, water resistant for many materials. Mix for use. Comes in five-minute or longer-setting varieties.
Liquid hide glue	Easier-to-use version of traditional hot hide glue. Long open (working) time. Heat and moisture weaken bond.
Modified PVA	Waterproof yellow glue. Withstands weather exposure, not submersion. Generally similar to yellow glue.
Polyurethane	Expands in joint as it cures, so must be clamped. Strong, waterproof. Bonds wood, metal, plastics.
PVA (polyvinyl acetate)	White glue. Strong, not waterproof. Long open time. Joints must fit well. Corrodes steel.

METRIC CONVERSIONS

U.S. UNITS TO METRIC EQUIVALENTS			METRIC EQUIVALENTS TO U.S. UNITS		
To Convert From	**Multiply by**	**To Get**	**To Convert From**	**Multiply by**	**To Get**
Inches	25.4	Millimeters	Millimeters	0.0394	Inches
Inches	2.54	Centimeters	Centimeters	0.3937	Inches
Feet	30.48	Centimeters	Centimeters	0.0328	Feet
Feet	0.3048	Meters	Meters	3.2808	Feet
Yards	0.9144	Meters	Meters	1.0936	Yards
Square inches	6.4516	Square centimeters	Square centimeters	0.1550	Square inches
Square feet	0.0929	Square meters	Square meters	10.764	Square feet
Square yards	0.8361	Square meters	Square meters	1.1960	Square yards
Acres	0.4047	Hectares	Hectares	2.4711	Acres
Cubic inches	16.387	Cubic centimeters	Cubic centimeters	0.0610	Cubic inches
Cubic feet	0.0283	Cubic meters	Cubic meters	35.315	Cubic feet
Cubic feet	28.316	Liters	Liters	0.0353	Cubic feet
Cubic yards	0.7646	Cubic meters	Cubic meters	1.308	Cubic yards
Cubic yards	764.55	Liters	Liters	0.0013	Cubic yards

To convert from degrees Fahrenheit (F) to degrees Celsius (C), first subtract 32, then multiply by $5/9$.

To convert from degrees Celsius to degrees Fahrenheit, multiply by $9/5$, then add 32.

HOW TO USE THIS BOOK

There's no doubt about it; windows and doors can be challenging do-it-yourself projects. For example, installing a new prehung door requires demolition skills as well as an understanding of framing, an ability to install weatherproof flashing, and the skill to install finished-looking trim indoors and out. In fact, finally fastening the door into place is the easy part; the preparation and finishing touches require the most skill and patience.

Even repair and maintenance can be demanding—you'll often find weatherstripping and gaskets hard to replace, opening mechanisms balky, broken glass panes difficult to remove, and new panes tricky to cut.

That's why remodeling contractors charge a lot for anything to do with windows and doors. That's also why handling your own repair, upgrade, or installation is a prime opportunity for you to build some sweat equity.

Cutting the job down to size
This book is designed to provide you with clear, illustrated steps so you can handle such jobs yourself—and keep most of those remodeling bucks in your own pocket. For a good example of how this book takes challenging tasks and breaks them down into manageable stages, jump ahead to the chapter "Installing New Windows" beginning on page 86. You'll find that even installing a window where there was no window before is a doable project you can complete in a couple of weekends. Cover the bases each step of the way and you'll end up with a completed project you can be proud of.

Getting started
If you are contemplating adding a new window or door, get off to a good start with the first chapter, "Planning Windows & Doors." It demonstrates that windows and doors have the power to transform your home. For a look at the possibilities, check the galleries on pages 8–11 and 18–19. This chapter will also help you understand the various types and styles you can choose from, and the pros and cons of the materials that are used for windows and doors.

Tailored to your situation
Stanley Complete Doors & Windows is essentially two books in one, so whether your primary project is a window or a door, you won't have to jump all over the book to get the job done. And because your home likely has unique characteristics, you may run into situations unlike those shown in the step-by-step projects. When you encounter a difference, check the lower half of the page for boxes that provide more information. Boxes labeled "What If…?" present alternative solutions that you can apply to your specific situation.

You'll also find valuable expert advice and inside information on new tools and products in the "Stanley Pro Tip" boxes. "Safety First" boxes offer reminders on how to keep your project injury-free. Additional boxes and sidebars offer detailed information that can move your project along.

Knowing your limits
In addition to helping you through projects one step at a time, this book can give you an overview that will tell you what is—or isn't—within your do-it-yourself comfort zone. It may convince you that for major installations your role will be that of knowledgeable project manager. Fair enough; for the price of a roll of adhesive flashing you've got a book that will add to your knowledge base, putting you in a position to farm out the stuff you don't have the time or skills to take on.

PLANNING
WINDOWS AND DOORS

Adding a window or door can dramatically improve the appeal of a home, from the inside and outside. Windows and doors are architectural elements that can enhance a home and boost its resale value.

In addition to improving a home's appearance, windows and doors have a practical function. A window keeps out the elements while providing light. It may also frame an attractive view. If openable, it offers ventilation. A new door can change traffic patterns, easing movement through the house and eliminating bottlenecks. Patio or French doors are windowlike in their ability to frame new vistas. That's why doors and windows are popular do-it-yourself projects: They offer benefits in form and function.

This chapter introduces you to the types of windows and doors available and the materials from which they are made, and shows how you can make intelligent choices about which are best for you.

Choosing windows
Windows offer an extraordinary range of shapes, sizes, and materials, all with energy-efficient glazing. They come in a variety of styles (see pages 12–13) that can open by sliding up, down, or sideways or on hinges at the top, bottom, or side. Various millwork styles are available in such materials as wood, vinyl, and wood clad with aluminum or fiberglass (see page 14). Even if you are merely replacing windows without changing the size of the rough opening, you'll be able to choose

from many types of muntin and grill patterns. If you are installing a window where there was none before, you'll find the options almost overwhelming.

Selecting doors
A beautiful front entry door has long been synonymous with curb appeal; a carefully chosen interior door can do a lot to boost the attractiveness of a room. But beyond offering good looks, doors can be great problem solvers. Bifold, sliding, and pocket doors are real spacesavers; patio and French doors can provide plenty of room for party-level traffic. Like windows, doors are now available in a wide range of materials (see pages 22–23) in a range of prices.

Take advantage of the options in style, materials, and affordability.

CHAPTER PREVIEW

Windows make a difference
page 8

Window types and styles
page 12

Selecting window materials
page 14

Doors that open new possibilities
page 18

Use that camera
If you have a digital camera and a printer, you have a valuable planning aid at your disposal. Print out views of your home, attach tracing paper, and sketch out window and door locations and styles.

Take plenty of time to plan; windows and doors are costly and often must be ordered in advance. To aid your selection, gather catalogs and literature from home centers or the Internet.

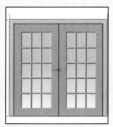

Door types and styles
page 20

Tools to use
page 24

Demolition and patching techniques
page 26

WINDOWS MAKE A DIFFERENCE

Whether you are upgrading a single window or choosing several windows for an addition, make the most of the opportunity to enhance your home. Often the transformation can be modest; a new muntin or grill treatment can transform even a humble replacement window into an eye-catching feature. On a larger scale, combining individual windows into a grouping can enhance the interior of a room and dramatically improve the exterior of your home at the same time.

Energy efficiency

The energy efficiency (see pages 16–17) of modern glazing comes close to making windows more an energy asset than an energy drain. That means you can use them to full effect to make memorable rooms. But bigger windows are not always better.

A small window positioned over a door as a transom or set high in a wall can offer ambient light and just the right touch of architectural interest.

Windows are a principal source of light and a view out, but they also provide ventilation. The nearer the ceiling, the more likely they are to allow warm air to flow out, which lets cool air move in through lower windows.

A simple window, combined with a built-in window seat, can make a cozy nook for relaxing (above). An old idea whose time has come again, transom windows over doors (above right) provide ventilation. A wall of muntin windows (right) is always dramatic.

Making the best of your choice

An off-the-shelf window can be substantially upgraded if you take extra effort with the casing and trim. Think in terms of combining windows with built-ins. For example, when combined with a dormer window seat, even a simple square window (facing page) becomes a lovely feature. Windows can also have a powerful effect when paired with new cabinets or shelves.

If you have a view to emphasize, there's an ideal window for it. If the windows will be positioned near an area where you will spend a lot of time (such as the kitchen), all the better.

Light, ventilation, and a view are the things windows offer; how those benefits are put to use is up to you. For example, openable windows placed over a living area (above) move hot air out while providing soft ambient light. Skylights often work where wall space is limited (right).

Architectural versatility

Most window types can fit into a variety of architectural styles. Compare the rooms shown here—each of which tends toward the traditional—to the more contemporary examples shown on pages 8–9. Notice the windows themselves. Surprisingly, the same types are used successfully in very different architectural contexts. Placement, trim, and window treatment set the style, not the window types themselves.

Bays, bows, and bumpouts

Bay and bow windows (see page 13) are ideal for traditional homes. Both can be ordered ready-made and installed without much more difficulty than any other large window. A bumpout—a variation on the bay or bow—uses individual window units set into a frame, often with a cantilevered floor. It can increase the floor area in a room without the expense of adding an extension

Awning and casement windows combine to make an appealing corner installation (right). A bay window affords a wide vista (below) while providing architectural interest. Sometimes understatement says it all; a round window is elegantly simple (below right).

to the foundation. Window installation in a bumpout is standard; it is the framing that is the challenge.

Location, location

Window placement in a traditional home tends toward the symmetrical. Groupings tend to be centered in a wall or positioned in a corner. Individual windows can be a powerful, traditional touch. A single full-round window (facing page) set in a gable or dormer has long been used to add visual punch and soften the squares and rectangles that otherwise dominate. Placing a single square window on point (below) calls to mind an Amish quilt pattern.

Placement includes the ceiling as well. Skylights (see page 13) can suit any style of home. When placed on the northern side of the house, they provide steady ambient daylight. In many situations skylights become nearly invisible sources of light, which means they will meld well with windows of any style.

A Palladianlike grouping of windows (top) has a timeless traditional appeal, even when combined with skylights. Even a single window placed in an unusual way can make a strong statement (left), as can a set of simple windows nicely trimmed (above).

WINDOW TYPES AND STYLES

If you are replacing a window, it may be best for consistency's sake to buy a unit similar to other windows in the room. But there are many good reasons to take advantage of another of the variety of window types. For example, casement windows offer the greatest ventilation area and seal tightly against the weather. Bay and bow windows and, to a degree, garden windows, provide the illusion of additional space in a room. Fixed windows, of which the picture window is the most common variation, leave no doubt about sealing out the elements. Large ones offer an unimpeded view; small ones look great in gables and other out-of-the-way places.

Style considerations
Some windows are associated with a particular architectural style. For example, double-hung windows are expected in traditional homes; fixed windows are associated with contemporary homes. However most of these types can be added to any architectural style. Muntins and grills can be used, along with interior and exterior trim, to integrate the unit with the style of your home.

Standard window types
Double-hung windows were invented to provide convenient ventilation; the top sash can be lowered to let warm air escape and the bottom sash raised to let in cool air. Today the top sash is often fixed and the lower sash is smaller; with air-conditioning, windows are usually opened only in early spring and late autumn. **Sliding windows** are much like double-hung windows laid on their side. They are easy to open and simple to maintain.

A **casement window** swings out like a door to let in cooling breezes. Often a bay or bow

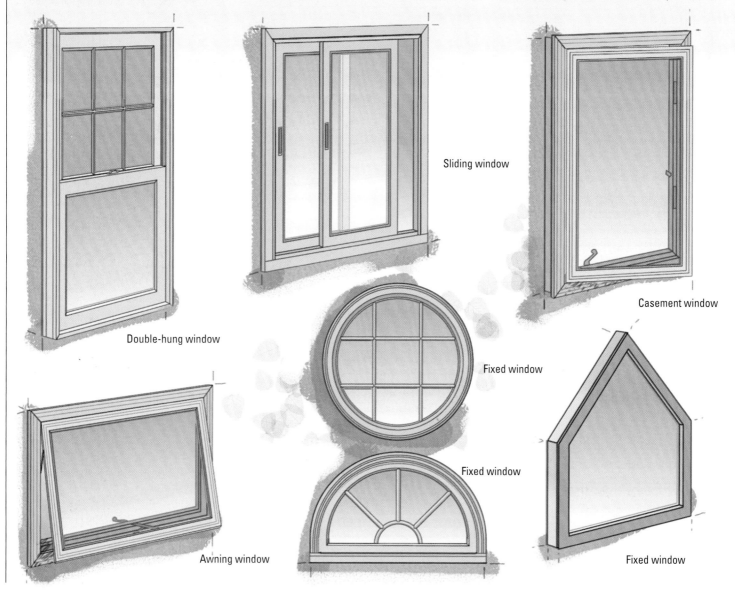

Double-hung window

Sliding window

Casement window

Fixed window

Awning window

Fixed window

Fixed window

window will include casements at each side.
Awning windows provide somewhat less
ventilation area but offer the advantage of
protecting the interior from rain while the
window is open. A hopper window is hinged
at the bottom and opens inward.

   Fixed windows can offer large, unimpeded
views. Smaller units are great for hallways
or closets, where ventilation is not important.
They come in a variety of shapes and are
often combined with openable windows to
make a dramatic window grouping.

Window combinations

Bay windows add visual interest to a home's
exterior and give the illusion of expanded
space indoors. The deep sill makes a cozy
seating area or a shelf for plants. Bay
windows are manufactured ready to install.
Bow windows are made of four or more
windows set together in a gentle curve.
Both types can combine fixed and openable
windows. In a similar vein **garden windows**
bumpout to make a mini greenhouse that,
while often a welcome addition to a kitchen,
can provide space for plants in any room
of the house. Usually equipped with two

shelves, garden windows can be ordered
with openable side windows.

Options overhead

Skylights provide pleasant overhead light
and are ideal for spaces in the central
core of a home that have no wall windows.
They are also ideal for stairways, halls, and
bathrooms. Skylights are available with fixed
panes or openable, screened units. A **tubular
skylight** pulls in light with less installation
hassle than a skylight.

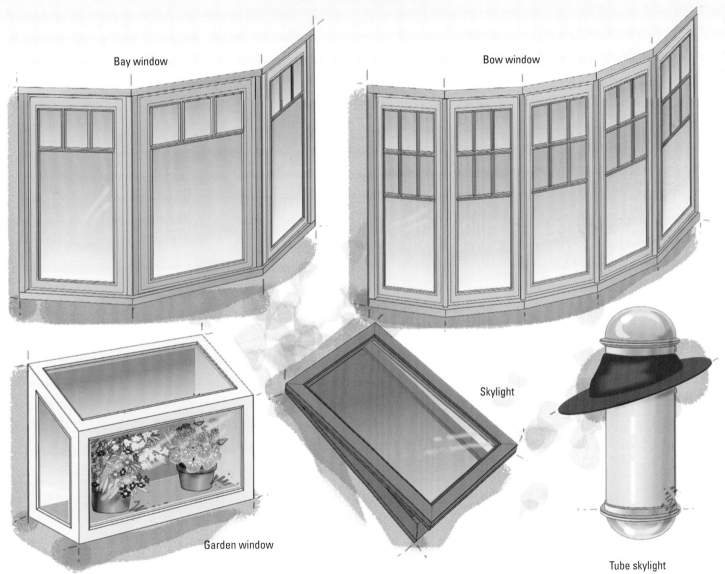

Bay window

Bow window

Garden window

Skylight

Tube skylight

SELECTING WINDOW MATERIALS

In addition to choosing your window's style and type of operating mechanism, there are other practical decisions to make. In general you will pay more for a window that has greater insulating properties and a greater ability to hold up against the elements. It is usually most cost-effective in the long run to install the best window you can afford.

Window frames can be made of wood (which may be clad with aluminum or vinyl on the exterior portions), vinyl, fiberglass, or metal. Higher-quality (and generally costlier) windows have better weatherstripping to keep air from filtering in around the sashes. The window glass may be single-, double-, or even triple-paned, and it may be treated with a coating that keeps warmth inside during the winter and outside during the summer.

Nearly every window seals out wind when the temperature is comfortable. But when the mercury drops well below freezing, many types of weatherstripping shrink and stiffen, becoming brittle and eventually cracking. This compromises the window's seal. Only the highest-quality windows perform well when temperatures drop below 0°F.

Consult with a knowledgeable salesperson at a home center or window supply source to choose the best window for your situation and budget. "Factors to look for" on the opposite page gives some of the performance values to consider.

Select and order your windows as early as possible. The least expensive windows come in standard sizes, which you may be able to simply pick up at a home center or window and door supply source. (See page 76 for instructions on measuring window size.) Custom windows cost more and may take several weeks to arrive. If the window is delivered with a flaw, is damaged in shipment, or is the wrong size (as can happen), you will have to reorder.

Fiberglass windows
In addition to the materials shown on these pages, some manufacturers make fiberglass windows. Fiberglass is stronger than vinyl, less prone to contracting and expanding, and less likely to warp. It needs to be protected by paint, but manufacturers apply a hard finish at the factory.

Vinyl window: This is usually the least expensive choice and is suitable for many applications. In lower-quality models, the weatherstripping (which is typically fuzzy) is not durable, and some of the plastic parts may break, especially when the window is tilted out for cleaning. Vinyl contracts and expands with changing temperatures, which reduces its ability to seal. It can also warp if exposed to very hot sunlight. Vinyl can be painted (it helps to apply alcohol-base primer first), but the paint may peel and need to be reapplied after a few years.

Wood window: Wood generally costs more than vinyl, and it periodically needs to be sealed with paint or finish to prevent rotting and sun damage. However, wood has natural insulating properties, and most people prefer the way it looks. Some are made with stain-quality wood, but windows that use wood with obvious joints will not look good stained; plan to paint instead.

Clad window: To make a wood window more durable, many manufacturers apply a cladding of aluminum, vinyl, or fiberglass to the exterior portions only. Aluminum cladding can be painted, as long as you first apply a primer. In most cases, tinted vinyl and fiberglass can be painted with no problem, but paint may have trouble sticking to white vinyl. You can also buy windows with hard-baked paint finishes.

Factors to look for

Most windows bear a rating sticker that gives performance scores for at least some of the following factors:

■ **R-value** measures the window's ability to prevent heat transfer—how it keeps uncomfortable temperatures outside and comfortable temperatures inside. The higher the R-value, the better.

■ **U-value** (or U-factor) is essentially the inverse of the R-value; it measures the tendency to transfer heat. So the lower the U-value, the better. (See map on page 16.)

■ **Solar gain** (also called solar heat gain coefficient, or SHGC) indicates how much the window will heat a room when the sun is shining. Solar gain is a good thing when the weather is cold, but it can definitely raise air-conditioning costs during the summer. The higher the number, the greater the heat gain. (See map on page 16.)

■ **Wind resistance,** or air leakage, is measured in cubic feet per minute (cfm). There should be two numbers: one for 70°F and one for 0°F. The lower the numbers, the better the seal.

A double-hung window (right) is the most common type, because of its versatility and ease of operation. It has a number of specialized parts. An exterior sill is slightly sloped so water can run off. The interior stool (often called the inside sill) is typically just wide enough for a small plant; if it were wider, people would bump into it. Stop moldings and parting stops must be precisely aligned so they can seal the window, yet allow sashes to slide up and down easily. The weight-and-pulley system shown here is typical of older wood windows; newer windows use friction or springs (see page 42) to keep the sashes in place when they are raised.

THE PARTS OF A DOUBLE-HUNG WINDOW

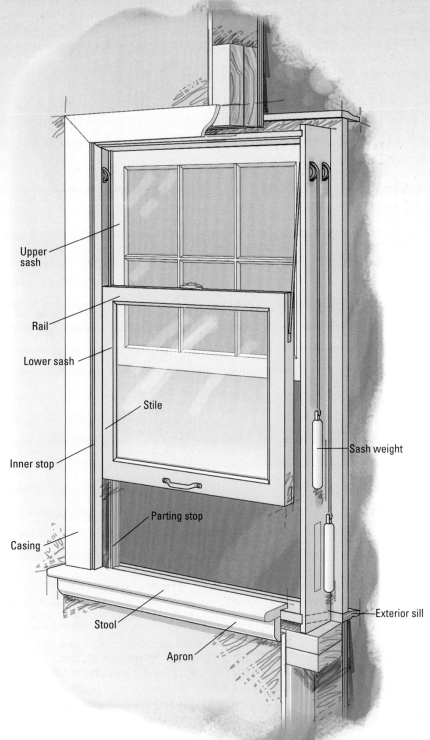

Upper sash

Rail

Lower sash

Stile

Inner stop

Sash weight

Parting stop

Casing

Stool

Apron

Exterior sill

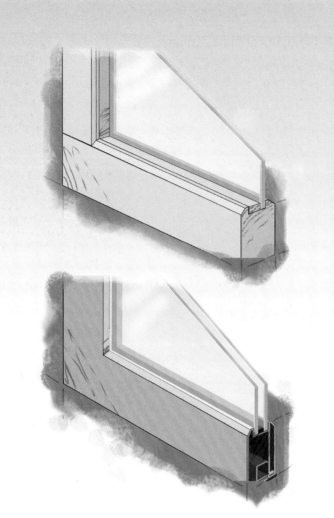

The right window for your region

In northern climates sealing out cold is the primary concern; in southern areas there is more concern for keeping out the heat. This map gives a general idea of the types of windows that are appropriate for each region; consult local window dealers for more specific recommendations. U-factor refers to rate of heat transfer; solar gain refers to the heat that penetrates the glass.

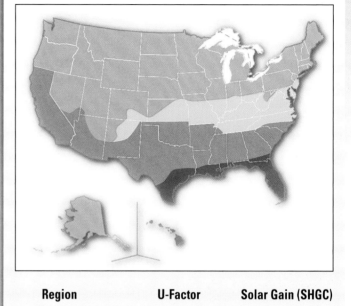

Region	U-Factor	Solar Gain (SHGC)
Northern Zone	0.35 or lower	no requirement
North/Central Zone	0.40 or lower	0.55 or lower
South/Central Zone	0.40 or lower	0.40 or lower
Southern Zone	0.40 or lower	0.65 or lower

Types of glazing

Single-glazed windows, with a single pane of glass in each sash, are the most affordable type, but they allow plenty of heat transfer, making for hefty heating and air-conditioning costs. In an older window the pane is usually held in place with glazing compound (putty) on the outside. With newer windows snap-in molding pieces take the place of the putty.

A double-glazed pane, also called insulating glass (IG) or thermal glass, dramatically increases a window's energy efficiency. The two panes are sealed with an air space between them that creates the insulation. The thicker the air space, the greater the insulation.

Triple-glazed windows, with three panes and two air spaces, are also available. These are not common, because the extra insulation they offer is not generally considered worth the significant extra cost.

You can increase a double-pane's energy insulation by ordering it with argon or krypton gas between the panes rather than air. Gas-filling usually costs more and can add to delivery time. The gas will leach out, but very slowly; after 20 years the pane will retain 90 percent of its original gas.

SAFETY FIRST
Tilt-out windows

Many windows tilt out for easy cleaning from the inside. Beware, however, of cheap windows with this feature; the hardware could break while you tilt them out and snap them back in.

STANLEY PRO TIP: **The benefits of low-E glass**

Glass with a low-emissivity (or low-E) coating admits direct solar heat but blocks long-wave heat reflected from driveways, buildings, and other surfaces. This reduces the total heat gain in a room. It also keeps out ultraviolet (UV) rays that fade furniture.

There are various types of low-E coatings; consult your window dealer to determine the best type for your location. Different coatings can allow high, moderate, or low solar heat gain. In hot climates a low-gain coating reduces passage of direct and reflected heat into the house. In cold climates a high-gain coating allows more solar heating. Coatings also block heat loss through the window from inside the house.

Low-E coating is usually invisible, but because it slightly reduces the amount of visible light that passes through the glass, it can make the glass appear to be tinted. Some low-E coatings reduce the view at night.

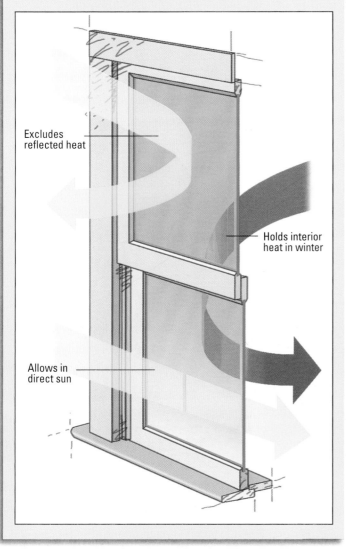

Excludes reflected heat

Holds interior heat in winter

Allows in direct sun

Flanged and block frames

A flanged window attaches to the house with a flange that is nailed or screwed to the exterior sheathing (see pages 104–105). A block-framed window has no flange and slides into an opening. It is the right choice when you want to install a replacement window in an existing frame (pages 76–79).

Removable grids

A removable grid attaches over a single pane to provide the look of an old-fashioned window or door with muntins and many small panes of glass. The grid lifts off so cleaning the window is far easier.

STANLEY PRO TIP: **The value of storm windows**

A well-made and tightly installed storm window can do wonders for an old window, greatly increasing its insulating properties by trapping several inches of air thickness between the window and the storm window. See pages 68–71 for instructions on choosing and installing storm windows.

DOORS THAT OPEN NEW POSSIBILITIES

Perhaps it's time to replace some old hollow-core doors in some bedrooms. Or maybe you want to trade your weary patio door for French doors with grill window dividers. Or is a weather-beaten entry door detracting from the appearance of your home? More than ever before, you can choose from doors and related hardware in an astonishing variety of styles, materials, and costs.

Grand entryways

A beautiful door, perhaps flanked by sidelights, makes a positive welcoming impression. Such elegance need not be expensive. Consider the simple panel door below. A careful paint job and some quality hardware make it a stylish entry. For modern architecture a simple flush door (right) with

a nicely finished birch or white oak veneer delivers understated elegance.

An upgraded entryway boosts your home's curb appeal. Real estate agents know the importance of first impressions. The front door not only is a focal point of your home's street face, it is the first part of your home a visitor sees up close.

Interior solutions

Inside your house, doors ensure privacy and sound buffering. They can add to the style and appeal of rooms as well. A pair of French doors (or sliding patio doors with divided lights like a pair of French doors) can be a beautiful feature. Even humble passage doors when combined with transoms (see page 8) can look great and have the added function of admitting light. Interior doors with

A grand entrance has long been emphasized in older homes, often leading to a dynamic partnership between the window and door (left). A contemporary approach goes for simplicity with a flush door (top). Pocket doors bring stage curtain drama to interior passageways (above).

frosted glass can maintain privacy without creating a closed-off feeling.

Cost considerations

A tight budget doesn't rule out a better entry. Rehabbing an existing door with paint and new hardware is an affordable approach. Or add an interesting window (called a door light) to a plain door. At the other end of the price range, you'll pay most for doors with sidelights and beveled glass, carved doors, or doors made of exotic woods. An upgraded entry is an investment you are unlikely to regret.

A plain door with a jolt of color (above left) dresses up a country home. Rich molding, brass fittings, and a leaded-glass window help the entry door (at left) measure up to its setting. Craftsman-style doors (above) are widely available.

DOOR TYPES AND STYLES

Ahome center or door specialty store will have a wide array of doors from which to choose. These two pages introduce you to the basic styles; pages 22 and 23 help you understand how the doors are built.

The hinged single door is the most common type. The room design must allow space for hinged doors to swing. Interior doors typically are lightweight and have two hinges; exterior doors are heavy and often use three hinges. Interior doors are usually 1⅜ inches thick, and exterior doors are commonly 1¾ inches thick.

A **panel door** is a classic style. It usually has three or four horizontal rails and three vertical stiles. The spaces between them are filled with thinner panels. Decorative molding (or some representation of it) called "sticking" surrounds each panel. The result is a richly textured look that is at home in both traditional and modern settings.

A **flush door** is a simple flat slab. It is usually the least expensive choice. If the surface is a hardwood veneer (usually birch or oak), a flush door can be stained, but other materials usually look best painted. Flush doors blend well with contemporary settings, but may look out of place in a traditional home. Interior flush doors are often hollow core, while exterior flush doors have a solid core and may have a metal or fiberglass face rather than wood veneer.

A pair of **French doors** adds a charming touch as well as an extra-wide doorway opening. These doors are almost always traditional in design. Often they have glass panels. They are most commonly used as exterior patio doors, but interior French doors can make a stunning passageway between rooms.

Many older homes have interior **pocket doors,** which slide into the wall when fully opened. They allow you to completely open the doorway without taking up any floor space. Pocket doors are making a

INTERIOR DOORS

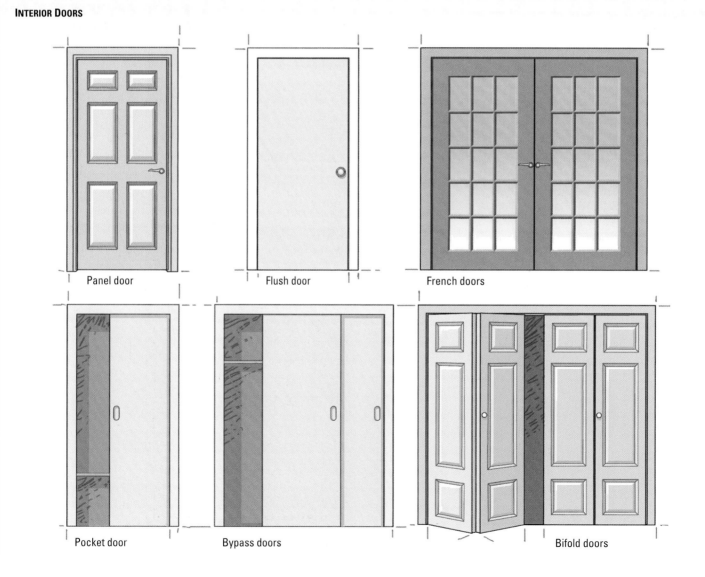

Panel door

Flush door

French doors

Pocket door

Bypass doors

Bifold doors

comeback; many styles are available, single and double. A pocket door requires wall space that cannot have electrical or plumbing lines running through it.

For a closet that is 6 feet wide or wider, a pair of **bifold doors** is the most popular choice. Each door takes up about half the swinging space of a hinged door. Bifolds can be flush, paneled, or louvered.

Somewhat less common are **bypass doors.** These operate much like sliding patio doors but are far lighter in weight. They are generally flush doors.

Entry doors can be made of wood, metal, or fiberglass. They range from straightforward

panel doors to **windowed doors** (the windows are sometimes referred to as "lights"), with attractive muntins or removable grills. Increasingly you can find **decorative carved-wood doors**. These often have rails and stiles with a carved section in the middle. They are expensive but make a memorable impression.

Even the most tightly sealed entry door can benefit from the addition of a **storm door.** These are usually made of metal or vinyl, but wood models are also available. A security storm door can be locked to keep out intruders and may be heavier than a standard door. Self-storing storm doors

have a window and screen. Inexpensive storm doors are often plain in design and can detract from the appearance of an entry door. You can pay more for a storm door that makes a design statement of its own, but perhaps the best choice is a storm door that unobtrusively frames your entry door.

Patio sliding doors are typically made of large panes of glass encased in wood, vinyl, or metal frames. They are the ideal choice when you want to maximize your view of the yard. Compared with French doors they take up no floor space when open. A possible disadvantage is that they only open half as wide as the doorway.

EXTERIOR DOORS

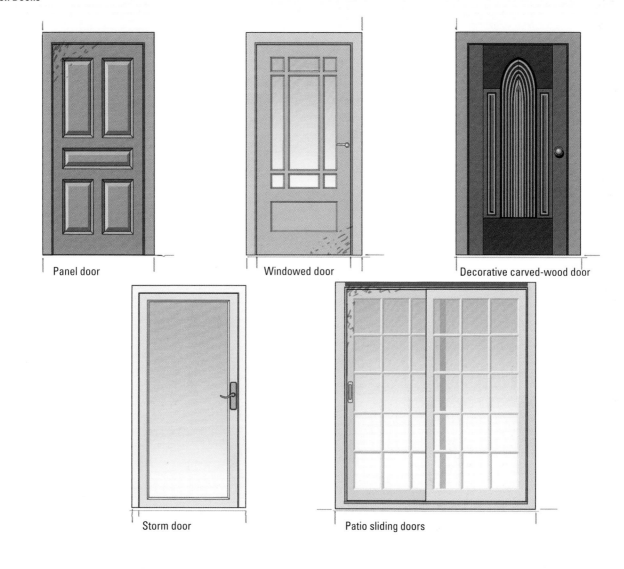

Panel door

Windowed door

Decorative carved-wood door

Storm door

Patio sliding doors

DOOR MATERIALS

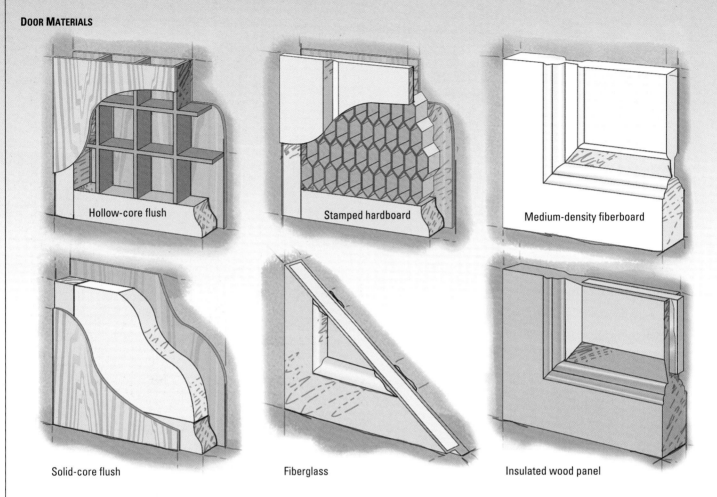

Hollow-core flush

Stamped hardboard

Medium-density fiberboard

Solid-core flush

Fiberglass

Insulated wood panel

Choosing door materials

Because wood has a tendency to warp and to expand and contract with the weather, a door cannot be made from a single slab of wood. Centuries of experience have resulted in the practice of making doors from interlocking pieces. On a panel door you can see the rails, stiles, and panels. But even flush doors have frames and fill-in pieces, all covered by a solid piece of veneer. Some materials perform better than others; check a door's construction to be sure it will meet your needs.

Interior doors are protected from the weather so they can be made of less-substantial materials than exterior doors. Never use an interior door for an exterior entryway. No matter how well you protect the door with paint, it will warp and come apart in a few years.

A **hollow-core flush interior door** is a common choice for new construction. It has a frame made of solid wood boards that are typically about 1½ inches wide. A cardboard webbing runs through the interior to provide rigidity and prevent drumming. These doors can last for decades if treated gently, but can be dented or punctured if hit hard. A door with a lauan mahogany veneer is the least expensive but will soak up paint like a sponge. It often pays in the long run to buy a door with oak or birch veneer.

Often the most affordable choice is a **stamped hardboard interior door.** The hardboard (sometimes called by the brand name Masonite) is a fairly soft material, but is usually covered with a hard-baked paint. The hardboard can be molded into a convincing approximation of natural wood grain. Some hardboard doors are hollow-core, while others are filled with foam or particleboard. These can look great for years if treated gently, but they are easily dented; if they become wet for prolonged periods, the hardboard will swell. Both conditions are difficult to repair.

Interior doors made of **medium-density fiberboard (MDF)** are gaining in popularity. Many of these doors have a paneled yet modern look and are available in a wide range of attractive styles. MDF is harder and less susceptible to denting than hardboard, though not as strong as solid wood.

A **solid-core flush exterior door** is made much like a hollow-core interior door, but the space within the wood frame is filled with solid particleboard. These are very heavy but not as durable as other exterior doors. If not kept protected with paint, the veneer may delaminate from the particleboard. And if the particleboard gets wet, the door can become unusable.

Fiberglass exterior doors are quickly gaining in popularity. Fiberglass is easily molded into most any shape and style. Fiberglass is durable, hard, and not prone to shrinking, expanding, or warping. These doors are available in a variety of colors and are easy to paint.

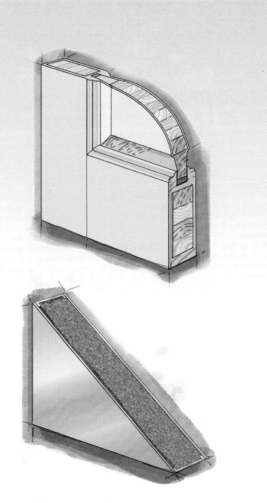

Glass doors

Wood-panel doors, made for interior and exterior applications, have a classic appeal. Solid wood has good strength and insulating properties. Hardwoods such as oak are very resistant to denting; softwoods such as pine are more easily dented but are still quite durable. You'll pay more for a stain-grade door, which is made of full-length attractive pieces of wood. A paint-grade door joins together smaller pieces. All exterior doors must be protected with paint or finish to prevent them from warping or cracking. Some exterior wood-panel doors have a foam core, for added insulation and stability.

A **stave-core** (also called "core-block") **exterior door** looks like a standard wood-panel door, but it is made of several thin pieces of wood that are laminated together. The laminated core is then covered with a wood veneer. This method makes for an extremely stable door. However the veneer is liable to peel if the door is not kept protected with stain or paint.

Once considered an option only for commercial applications, **steel exterior doors** are increasingly popular for homes. Some have a steel face with a foam core for insulation. Others have a core made of foam wrapped in steel, with a wood veneer applied to the exterior. The result is a door with good insulating properties that is also very strong and burglar resistant.

Glass-paneled doors need to be well built, especially if they are exterior doors. Individual glass panes are often referred to as "lights" (or "lites"). Be sure to get gas-filled thermal glass panes for an exterior door (see page 16), and make sure the glass is well sealed against the stiles and rails.

TOOLS TO USE

Buy good-quality tools that feel solid and comfortable in your hand. A tool belt will keep many of the tools within easy reach.

Basic carpentry tools
A 1-inch-wide **tape measure** handles most measuring jobs. The hook on the end moves back and forth so you'll get accurate measurements when pushing on the blade for an inside measurement or pulling for an outside measurement. You'll also need

squares to ensure true right-angle corners, and a **level** to check for level and plumb. A **chalkline** quickly marks a long, straight line; a **straightedge** is handy as well.

For trim work a 16-ounce **hammer** is the usual choice. Also have on hand **nail sets** so you can finish driving nails without marring the wood. You'll need a **drill** to bore pilot holes. If it's a drill/driver with a **screwdriver bit,** you can use it to quickly drive screws too. A **flat pry bar** removes framing and trim;

a heavy-duty **pry bar** helps with demolition.

A **circular saw** handles rough and fairly fine cuts. Use **wood chisels** and a **utility knife** for small cutting jobs, such as making mortises for hinges. A **sanding block** will sand wood and filler smooth without making gouges caused by finger pressure.

For miscellaneous repairs and hardware installation, have a set of **screwdrivers** on hand and several kinds of **pliers**.

Sawhorses help with cutting and assembly.

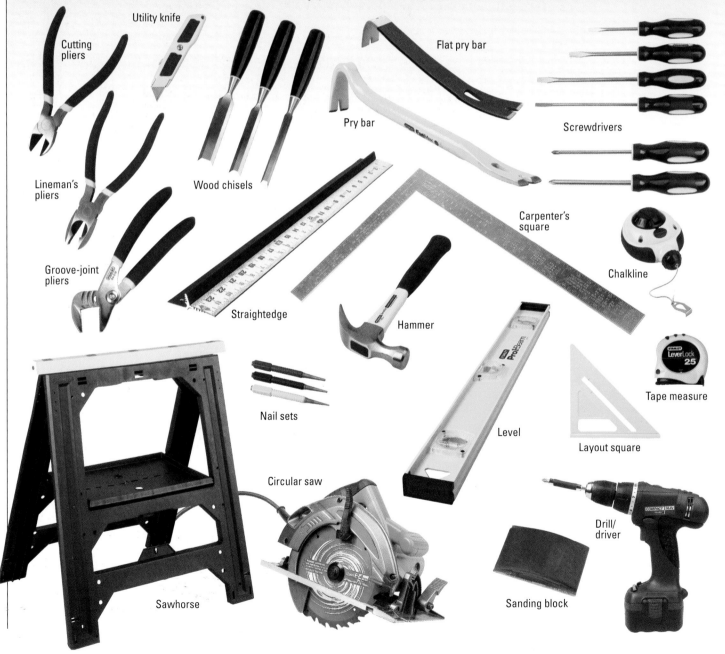

Utility knife

Cutting pliers

Flat pry bar

Lineman's pliers

Wood chisels

Pry bar

Screwdrivers

Carpenter's square

Groove-joint pliers

Chalkline

Straightedge

Hammer

Nail sets

Level

Tape measure

Layout square

Circular saw

Drill/ driver

Sawhorse

Sanding block

Special tools

You can make precise cuts with a **miter box and backsaw,** though a power mitersaw is faster and more accurate—it's worth the investment if you have lots of cutting to do. A **handsaw** is always useful. A **reciprocating saw** is indispensable for demolition work and for cutting openings. A **skill saw** makes precise curved cuts. Use a **hacksaw** to cut metal. A **nail puller** helps remove framing.

Unlike a hammer and nail set, a **pneumatic finish nailer** perfectly sets nails quickly, and there is no chance of marring the wood with a missed hammer blow. You'll need an air compressor to operate it. You can rent the nailer and a compressor.

A **stud sensor** detects the presence of metal or wood studs in the wall. A multisensor can also detect hidden wiring and plumbing lines.

For installing glass use a standard **putty knife**, a **glazier's putty knife,** or a **glazier's tool.** If you want to cut the glass yourself, you can do so with a simple **glass cutter.** Use a pull-type **paint scraper** to quickly remove old putty or strip away caked-on paint; a **wire brush** helps too. For installing flashing you'll need **tin snips** and a **stapler.**

Doors often need to be shaved to size. Use a **plane** or a **shaping tool.** A **butt-hinge marker** is the quickest and most accurate way to cut mortises for hinges; a **center marker punch** helps accurately drill holes for screws. When installing a new door handle or lock, you'll need correct-sized **drill bits** and **hole saws.**

Paint scraper

Putty knife

Glazier's putty knife

Wire brush

Center marker punch

Glass cutter

Stud sensor

Hole saw

Spade bit

Shaping tool

Tin snips

Glazier's tool

Stapler

Butt-hinge marker

Pneumatic finish nailer

Miter box and backsaw

Nail puller

Plane

Skill saw

Handsaw

Hacksaw

Reciprocating saw

DEMOLITION AND PATCHING TECHNIQUES

Remodeling work is more challenging than new construction because often you must cut the opening, reconfigure the framing, install the unit, then patch the walls on the inside and the outside to make it look like the new window or door was always there. The next six pages show some common demolition and patching methods.

Before you begin demolition, be sure to locate any electrical, plumbing, or low-voltage lines running through the section you plan to remove. If you are at all unsure of what you encounter, hire a professional contractor, at least as a consultant.

Electrical lines can usually be rerouted without a great deal of effort, but to do this yourself you must have an understanding of wiring methods. **Shut off the power to the circuit before touching the lines.**

Plumbing gets messier. Supply pipes can be moved fairly easily, but drain and vent pipes are usually difficult to reroute. The same applies for heating or air-conditioning ducts. If any of these obstacles are present, hire a plumber or find a new place to install the window or door.

STANLEY PRO TIP

Organizing the job site

If you have a large wall area to remove, consider renting a trash container. For smaller amounts contact your garbage company to see if, for an extra fee, they will haul it away. Otherwise, you may be able to pile the trash in your yard and set it out for garbage pickup a little at a time.

Demolition can produce a mighty mess, so take steps to keep the dust out of the rest of the house. Seal doorways with plastic (you may want to purchase a special plastic construction doorway, which has a zipper door). Place a fan blowing outdoors to remove some of the dust. Determine where you will throw the garbage, and cover the ground with a plastic tarp or sheets of plywood. Shovel smaller debris directly into a wheelbarrow or garbage bin.

Checking for utility lines

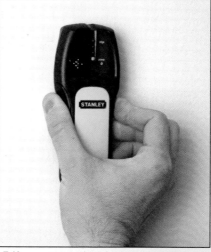

1 If you see an electrical receptacle or light switch in the area, you know there is wiring in the wall. Use a multisensor to detect electrical and plumbing lines. Also look in the basement directly below for plumbing lines and heat vents, which usually travel straight vertically. **CAUTION: Even if you are fairly certain that no lines are running through the wall, cut the interior wall carefully and slowly using hand tools, so you can stop if you feel a cable or pipe.**

2 If you have wiring knowledge and skills and need to remove an electrical line, **shut off the power to the circuit and test to be sure that power is off.** Disconnect the receptacle or switch, and pull the box out of the wall. For further instructions on running electrical lines, see *Stanley Complete Wiring.*

INSIDE THE WALLS

Drywall

Fiberglass

Chipboard

Building wrap

Lath

Plaster

Planks

Loose fill

Tar paper

Most walls are framed with 2×4 or 2×6 vertical studs spaced 16 or 24 inches apart. They have a bottom and a top plate. (An older balloon-framed home may not have bottom or top plates.) Drywall is the most common interior finish for post-World War II homes; lath and plaster is common for prewar homes.

Exterior walls usually have insulation, which may be fiberglass blankets or loose fill material. On the exterior there is usually sheathing, made with chipboard or particleboard for newer homes and planks in older homes. The sheathing is covered with felt (tar paper) or building wrap, then with siding.

Marking for cutting holes in walls

1 Use a stud sensor to locate the studs. Depending on the framing configuration you choose (see pages 89–95, 152–155, and 168–171), you may decide to move the door or window over a few inches to take advantage of an existing stud.

2 Mark the area you want to cut out. In some cases it makes sense to surgically remove only the area where the wall or door will go; you may be able to hide all the cuts with molding. In other cases you may choose to remove a larger area, and patch it after the installation.

3 To get a sense of how the installation will look from outside, drill locator holes through the outside wall at each corner. For a house with wood, vinyl, or aluminum siding, use a drill equipped with a long spade bit. For a stucco wall, finish the hole with a masonry bit.

Removing trim

1 The joint between a piece of molding and the interior or exterior wall may be sealed by paint. To avoid marring the paint on the adjoining wall, slice along the trim with a utility knife.

2 To pry off trim, tap a flat pry bar under the molding. Place a scrap of wood against the wall to act as a fulcrum and protect the wall from denting. Pry first with the long part of the pry bar, then with the shorter part.

Removing nails

If you want to reuse a piece of molding, pull the nails out through the back. This will leave the front of the piece free of holes. Firmly grab a nail with a pair of lineman's or slip-joint pliers and roll the pliers to remove the nail.

Cutting out drywall

1 Use a hand drywall saw to cut through drywall. (A circular saw cuts quickly but will raise clouds of dust; a jigsaw or reciprocating saw will raise less dust, but you will not be able to feel an electrical cable or plumbing pipe.) If you want a very clean cut, slice through the paper with a utility knife first, then cut along the inside of the knife line with the saw.

2 Punch a hole near a corner of the drywall with a hammer, then pry with a flat pry bar. Work carefully so you do not damage the adjoining wall. If the drywall was attached using construction adhesive, you may need to use a chisel to remove the drywall from the studs.

3 Once you have cut a hole or two, grab with your hands and pull. You may be able to remove the drywall in large pieces. Pull out or pound in all exposed nails. Remove insulation wearing gloves, long clothing, safety goggles, and a dust mask.

Cutting out plaster

1 To help keep the adjoining wall from cracking, apply masking tape (not blue painter's tape, which does not stick as well) just outside the cutline. Use a straightedge and utility knife to score the cutline repeatedly until you have cut through the plaster. You'll need to change blades often.

2 Place a drop cloth on the floor because you will generate plenty of debris. Gently tap with a hammer to break the plaster away from the lath on the inside of the area to be removed. Tap out most of the plaster between the lath pieces. Remove the plaster to a garbage container.

3 Peer between the lath to make sure there are no utility lines. Cut the lath using a reciprocating saw or a jigsaw. To keep the lath from vibrating and cracking the adjoining wall, press firmly against the wall and cut slowly. Pry the lath from the studs, and pry out or pound in the nails.

Removing wood siding

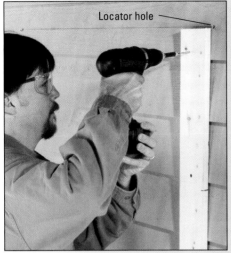

Locator hole

1 Drill locator holes from the inside to mark the four corners of the cutout. Use a pencil and straightedge or a chalkline to mark the siding. Temporarily attach a 1×4 guide board just inside a cutline.

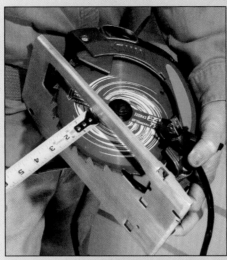

2 Set the saw blade to cut through the siding and the sheathing while the saw's base is resting on the guide board.

3 Holding the saw's base firmly against the guide board and watching that the blade moves right beside the guide board, cut along the lines. Stop at each corner.

4 Tap shims into the bottom cut so that the section will not slip down while you work. Finish the cuts at the corners using a reciprocating saw, jigsaw, or handsaw.

5 Remove the section. If the siding and sheathing are attached to an interior stud, have a helper pound out from the inside of the house while you hold the section.

STANLEY PRO TIP

Other wall-removal methods

If dust is not a problem (as when the house is vacant) and you are sure you will not run into utility lines, it is quicker to remove drywall or plaster using a circular saw.

It sometimes works to simply cut through the plaster and the lath at the same time using a jigsaw or reciprocating saw. Press firmly against the wall to prevent vibration that could crack the wall.

If drywall was attached using construction adhesive, you may need to chisel the drywall from the wood. You may choose to leave the drywall attached and cut through the studs to produce pieces small enough for the garbage.

Cutting out stucco

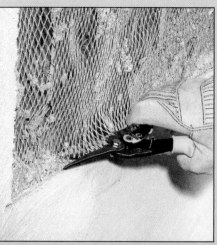

1 Drill locator holes at the corners. Use a pencil and a straightedge, or chalkline, to mark the cutlines. Equip a circular saw with a masonry-cutting blade and set it to a depth of about ½ inch. Wearing protective clothing and eyewear, cut along the lines. See that the blade cuts just through the stucco and metal lath, and not deeply into the sheathing. You will need to adjust the depth of the blade, which will wear down as you cut.

2 Use a hammer and cold chisel to finish the cuts at the corners. Tap with a small sledgehammer or a standard hammer to break the stucco from the wall. You will likely encounter two or three layers of stucco.

3 Use tin snips to cut away the wire lath where it has not already been cut. Pry away the nails holding the metal lath and discard the lath. You can now cut through the sheathing with a circular saw. If the sheathing is solid wood, you can cut a smaller opening in it so the window's flange can be attached to the sheathing.

Patching wood siding

1 You may need to cut back individual pieces of siding so you can "weave" in the patching pieces and avoid an odd-looking rectangular section. To do this, tap shims under the piece above, and cut using a keyhole saw. You may need to use a hacksaw blade or a mini hacksaw to cut through some nails.

2 Cover any exposed sheathing with pieces of roofing felt or building wrap. The new paper should overlap the old by at least 3 inches. Cut the bottom piece of siding to fit and slide it up and into place; you may need to pry out the piece above. Whenever possible position nails so they will be covered by the piece above.

3 Continue working up. Where you need to drive a nail near the end of a siding piece, drill a pilot hole first to prevent splitting the board.

Patching stucco

Stucco masking tape

1 When cutting a hole in stucco for a window, you'll often accidentally knock off more stucco than you intended or hit an already damaged patch. To make a repair, mask the installed window and use a wire brush to remove any loose stucco. You may have to add stucco mesh or hardware cloth.

2 Buy a container of stucco-patching compound. Use a trowel to press the first coat into the metal lath. It should be thick enough to cover the lath, but about ⅜ inch less thick than the surrounding area. Scratch a series of lines in the stucco and keep it moist for two days or so.

3 You may need to apply three coats, but two are usually enough. Before you apply the finish coat, practice on scrap wood to achieve the texture you desire (see below). Dampen the wall. Apply patching compound, then use the tool of your choice to produce the desired result. In this case a mason's brush is used to blend in the patch.

Working with vinyl siding

Vinyl and aluminum siding require a special edging for windows. Both can be cut with a utility knife or tin snips. Cut a siding patch 6 inches longer than the area so that it can overlap by 3 inches on each side. Also cut

off the nailing flange at the top. Apply polyurethane sealant or gutter caulk to the existing siding and press the patch piece into place. Tape it tightly onto the wall until the adhesive has set.

WHAT IF...
You need to match a stucco finish

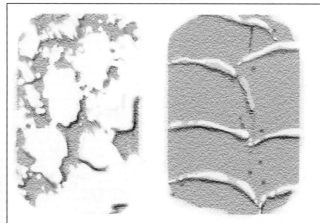

To make the texture above, pull the trowel away from the wall to make pronounced peaks. Gently scraping the peaks with a trowel will produce a mesalike

"knockdown" texture (above left). Or, working from the top of the patch, pivot the trowel on its base for an overlapping arc effect (above right).

WINDOW REPAIRS

You don't have to put up with a problem window that's hard to open, slams down unexpectedly, or leaks air. Most windows can be repaired so they operate as good as new.

Should you replace?

It is often assumed that an old double-hung wood window should be replaced in order to achieve long-term energy savings. Before you replace your venerable window, consider:

■ A double-hung window that uses chains or ropes attached to sash weights (see pages 40–41) may seem old-fashioned, but with maintenance every few decades this weight system can last for centuries. Newer windows are often more difficult to repair.

■ Older windows have single glazing, which does not insulate as well as double glazing. However, most energy loss is usually through gaps between sashes and the frame or between the frame and the house; energy loss through the glass is usually a lesser factor.

■ By adding a good-quality storm window, you can achieve much of the insulation of double glazing, plus extra protection against air infiltration through gaps. If you also take steps to weatherstrip your window (pages 58–61), you will end up with a window that seals at least as well as most new windows—at a fraction of the cost.

Starting with glass replacement this chapter will take you through all the basic repairs, both minor and major. You'll find instructions for restoring double-hung, sliding, and casement windows, as well as wood and metal storm windows.

Energy conservation is a major payoff for window fix-ups.

CHAPTER PREVIEW

Replacing glass
page 34

Repairing sash windows
page 38

Repairing casement windows
page 44

Repairing sliding windows
page 46

If one of your windows is losing its glazing and has cracked panes, chances are good that several others are in the same shape. Repairing them is an investment of true sweat equity. The cost of tools and materials is modest.

Screen and storm window repairs
page 48

Replacing windowsills
page 52

REPLACING GLASS

Replacing a broken single-glaze pane is messy and requires attention to detail, but with a bit of practice you can learn to install the glass safely and make smooth glazing lines. In most cases it is best to have a local hardware store or glass specialist cut the glass for you. (If you want to cut it yourself, see opposite page.)

Unless the pane is very small, order double-thick glass; single-thick glass breaks easily. In a door, sidelight, or other high-traffic areas, order shatter-resistant glass.

Be sure to wear thick gloves, long clothing, and protective eyewear when handling shattered glass. Tiny, nearly invisible splinters can cause injury.

Traditional glazing putty (also called glazing compound) is applied with a putty knife. You can also buy glazing putty in a caulk tube (see page 62), but applying with a knife creates a tighter bond and a smoother surface once you get the hang of it.

Often it is possible to replace double-glaze panes yourself; see the most common types of installation on page 36. In some cases you may need to take the sash into a hardware store or glass specialist for repairs.

PRESTART CHECKLIST

☐ **TIME**
1 or 2 hours to replace most types of windowpanes

☐ **TOOLS**
Tape measure, paint scraper, chisel, glazier's putty knife or standard putty knife, wire brush, heat gun, perhaps a glass cutter

☐ **SKILLS**
Measuring carefully, applying glazing putty

☐ **PREP**
Clear away shattered glass and place a drop cloth on the floor or ground below.

☐ **MATERIALS**
Glass pane to fit, glazing points, glazing compound (putty), linseed oil

Replacing glass in a wood frame

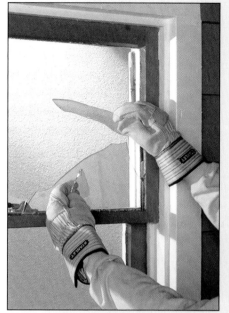

1 Usually you can replace glass while the sash is still in the frame, but it is easier to remove the frame first and work on a table. While wearing protective clothing, wiggle and pull out the shards of glass. You may need to tap the glass with a hammer to create a new break line first.

2 Take care to remove all pieces of glass, putty, and metal glazing points. You may need to use a pull-type paint scraper or an old chisel. If you use a hammer, tap gently. The grooves where the new window will go must be completely smooth. A heat gun can help soften the old putty.

WHAT IF...
The glass is cracked but not shattered?

If the glass does not easily pull out in pieces, apply a grid of duct tape to the pane. Use a heat gun and scraper or chisel to remove all the putty and points, and pull the pane out in one piece.

Make glazing invisible inside

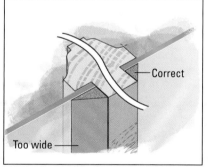

Correct

Too wide

If the glazing bead is too wide, it will be unpleasantly visible from the inside. Make sure the putty does not extend past the muntins or frame.

3 Wire-brush the frame and vacuum or wipe with a slightly damp rag. Apply a coat of linseed oil to the rabbet; this helps the putty stick securely.

4 Carefully measure the height and width of the opening in at least two places. Order (or cut yourself; see below) a piece of glass ⅛ inch shorter in each direction. Test-fit the pane before proceeding.

5 Roll a ball of glazing compound into a thin rope. Press it into the corner of the rabbet. Then use a putty knife to press it firmly into place, making a thin bed of putty for the glass to rest against.

6 Gently press the glass into the putty bed, checking that it lies flat against the rabbet in all places. Every 6 inches or so, press a glazing point into the wood; push only gently against the glass as you go.

STANLEY. PRO TIP: **Cutting your own glass**

If you want to cut your own glass, prepare a level table by spreading carpeting or sheets of newspaper. Measure and then mark the glass with a felt-tip pen. Place a straightedge about ⅛ inch from the line (to accommodate the thickness of the cutter) and apply a line of oil along the line. Position the cutter against the glass at the top and press firmly as you draw it down. You should hear a scratching noise—indicating that the glass is being etched—all along the line. (If there is a gap in the etching, scratch again, but it works best if you get it all in the first pass.)

Slip a wood dowel or thin piece of wood just under the cutline, and press on both sides to break the glass. If the edge is rough, smooth it with a sanding block.

Replacing glass in a wood frame *continued*

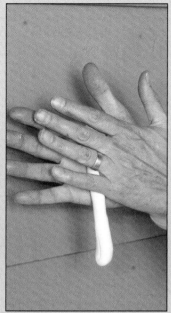

7 Roll a rope of putty about ¾ inch thick. Aim for a fairly uniform diameter, but it need not be perfect.

8 Press the rope against the glass and the frame, using your thumb. Using a rag to periodically apply linseed oil to a glazier's knife or putty knife, press again using swiping motions every inch or two.

9 Working in the same direction and holding the knife at the correct angle so the putty will not be visible inside (see page 34), press firmly and draw the knife along the line to smooth the putty.

10 If the resulting putty has a series of slight ridges, smooth them by lightly wiping with your finger, working in the opposite direction as in step 9.

Three types of glazing for thermal panes

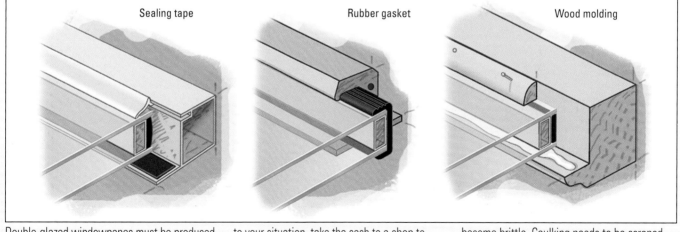

Sealing tape　　　　　　　Rubber gasket　　　　　　　Wood molding

Double-glazed windowpanes must be produced by a professional; you cannot cut them yourself. They are secured in a variety of ways. Here are the three most common methods. If the techniques on the opposite page do not apply to your situation, take the sash to a shop to have the glass replaced.

Sealing tape usually needs to be replaced. **Rubber gaskets** can often be reused, but only if they are unbroken and have not dried and become brittle. Caulking needs to be scraped away and replaced. **Wood molding** can usually be reused, but you may replace it with new molding.

Replacing glass in a vinyl frame

1 Use a putty knife or small flat pry bar to remove the vinyl stop. Work carefully, to avoid cracking the stop. Remove the glass and order a new piece to fit.

2 Test to see that the new pane will fit. Scrape away the old sealing tape and clean the surface with paint thinner. Cut pieces of sealing tape to fit precisely and press them into place on the rabbet. Just before installing the glass, spread a bead of silicone sealant onto the rabbet.

3 Carefully set the pane in place—you cannot adjust its position once it is set into the tape. Press the vinyl stop back into the frame to secure the glass.

Rubber gasket

If your pane is held in place with a rubber gasket, slip the gasket onto the edges of the glass, pressing firmly so the gasket is tight at all points. Then set the pane into the frame. You may need to partially disassemble the frame first.

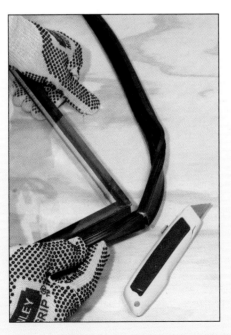

Wood molding

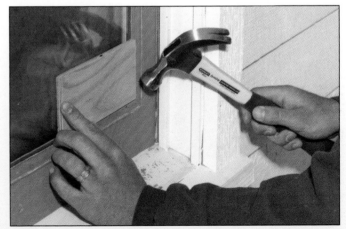

If a pane is secured with pieces of wood molding, pry the molding out with a small flat pry bar. Scrape away any old caulk, test the fit, and apply new silicone caulk. Press the pane into the caulk. When reinstalling the wood molding, take care to angle the nails so they do not touch the glass. (Reuse the old nail holes, perhaps driving slightly larger nails.) Use a scrap of plywood to protect the pane.

REPAIRING SASH WINDOWS

A double-hung wood window typically has two sashes that move up and down. Many people nail and paint shut the upper sash. This makes it easier to seal but will make cleaning the window difficult if you cannot get at it from the outside.

If a sash will not stay up, the chain or cord connecting to the weight is probably broken. Replacing a chain or cord can be accomplished in an hour or so.

To make an older unit work more smoothly, a bit of detailed work is often required. If the window has been painted many times, you may need to scrape or even remove paint from sashes or stops in order to free the action. A balky pulley may also need to have its paint removed. Often a spray lubricant will help as well.

A drafty window can be sealed by adding weatherstripping (see pages 58–61). A storm window (pages 68–71) will help greatly as well.

Newer windows have a variety of mechanisms to keep sashes up when raised. See page 42 for instructions about repairing the most common types.

PRESTART CHECKLIST

☐ **TIME**
1 or 2 hours for most repairs

☐ **TOOLS**
Screwdriver, hammer, utility knife, zipper tool, flat pry bar, tin snips, pliers, paint scraper, putty knife, taping blades, sanding block, chisel

☐ **SKILLS**
No special skills

☐ **PREP**
Place a drop cloth on the floor by the window.

☐ **MATERIALS**
Caulk, sash chain or cord, wire, spray lubricant, paraffin block or candle, finishing nails, perhaps repair parts for newer windows

Freeing a stuck sash

1 If a sash is painted shut, score the line with a zipper tool. You can use a utility knife, but the zipper cuts through paint with less chance of making a ragged edge.

2 If the sash remains stuck, wedge two taping blades or putty knives between the sash and the stop, insert a chisel or flat pry bar between them, and tap. Do this at several locations.

WHERE PROBLEMS DEVELOP

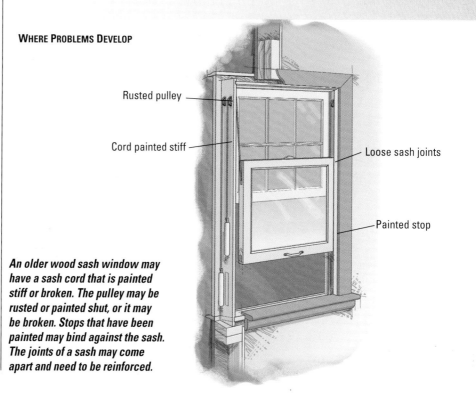

Rusted pulley

Cord painted stiff

Loose sash joints

Painted stop

An older wood sash window may have a sash cord that is painted stiff or broken. The pulley may be rusted or painted shut, or it may be broken. Stops that have been painted may bind against the sash. The joints of a sash may come apart and need to be reinforced.

3 If the window will not pull up by the handles, try prying it up. This is usually best accomplished from the outside. To protect against denting the wood, use two taping blades or putty knives and a pry bar. First try prying in the middle. If that doesn't work, pry one side, then the other.

4 Sashes glide through a channel formed by the jamb and stops. If these are caked with paint, use a pull-type paint scraper or a chisel to remove the impediments. Then sand or wire-brush and vacuum. For a really thorough job, remove the sashes and strip all the paint.

5 To make the window glide smoothly, lubricate the channel with candle wax, paraffin, spray silicone, or spray dry lube.

 **PRO TIP**

Setting straight an out-of-square window

If a sash doesn't align with the window frame (for example, if the gap is smaller at the bottom than the top), it is often the sash that is out of square. Remove the sash (see page 40), check it with a framing square, and repair as needed.

If the frame itself is out of square, the cause is likely the settling of the house. In this case, repairs are not easy. You'll have to remove the casing both inside and out and cut through the nails holding the window frame to the house's framing. Then you may be able to pry the frame into square and reattach it. If that is not achievable, you may be better off replacing the window—but be sure to address the house-settling problem first.

The sash binds against the stop?

If the sash binds against the stop, first try sanding the backside of the stop. If that does not solve the problem, remove the stop and reinstall it a bit farther from the sash—

or install a new stop. Close the sash, slip cardboard shims between the sash and the stop, and drive 3d finishing nails. (Do not reuse the old nail holes.)

Removing a sash and replacing cords or chains

1 If a sash cord or chain is broken, cut through the paint and pry out one or both of the stops. (If one cord is broken, it is a good idea to replace both at the same time.) Start prying in the middle and bend the stop out. (To do this for an upper sash, you will need to pull out the parting stop using pliers.)

2 Lift the lower sash and pull it out. To fix only one cord, you need only pull the window out on that side. (If the window has metal channels attached to the jambs, you will need to remove one or two nails or screws, and remove the channels along with the sash.)

3 To remove the access plate (which may be painted over and difficult to see), you may first have to remove a screw, then pry with a chisel. This gives you access to the cavity where the weights are.

WHAT IF...
You're using sash cord

1 To replace a sash cord, you may have to remove the pulley first and thread the cord through the pulley as shown. Tie a piece of string to the cord and attach a small weight such as a nail or a nut onto the other end of the string. Feed the cord into the cavity.

2 Attach the cord to the weight with a double or triple knot. Replace the weight in the cavity, pull the weight up several inches, and cut the cord about 2 inches below the sash hole (because you will tie a knot that will shorten the cord).

3 Tie a double knot and press the knot into the hole in the bottom of the sash channel. Drive a small nail or hole to ensure that the knot stays in place.

4 Insert one end of the sash chain into the pulley and thread it down until it reaches the bottom of the cavity. Some pulley mechanisms have a cover like this; others are open.

5 Pull the weight out through the access hole, cut the old cord, and remove it. Run the chain through the weight's hole and secure it with wire.

6 Put the weight back into the cavity. With the sash resting on the stool, pull on the chain until the weight lifts nearly to the pulley. Cut the chain right at the hole at the end of the groove.

7 Place the chain in the groove and drive two or three short screws to hold it in place. Make sure the screws are not long enough to hit the sash glass. Do the same on the other side when replacing both chains.

8 Set the sash back in place and test to see that it slides smoothly and stays open. With the sash fully closed, the weights should be at least 2 inches below the pulleys.

9 Reattach the stops. Drive slightly larger nails into the old holes, or drive 3d nails into new locations, using cardboard shims to keep the stop slightly away from the sash (see page 39).

Spiral balance

1 If the window has a spiral balance (see below) that is not holding the window, tilt out the sash to gain access to the slide where the bottom of the balance attaches. On some models you will need to remove the entire sash and disconnect the balance from the sash itself. Pry off any pieces that cover the balance.

2 Unhook the bottom of the spiral balance. Use a spiral balance tool to adjust the tension—usually it needs to be stronger in order to hold the window up.

3 If the balance is broken and you are unable to tighten it, remove and replace it with a balance of the same tension. If your home center does not carry the model you need, check specialty window stores or Internet sources.

FOUR SPRING SYSTEMS

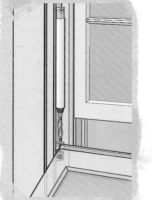

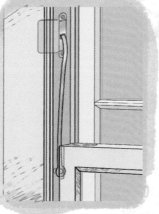

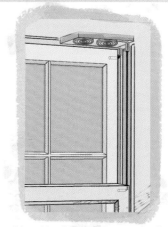

A spiral balance is encased for most of its length in a metal or vinyl tube. Twisting the bottom of the balance will increase or reduce the tension.

A block-and-tackle system has a nylon string line that attaches near the top of the window frame and runs into a spring that is encased in a metal sleeve. The spring connects to a sliding bracket that connects to the window. If problems develop, remove and replace the assembly.

A clockspring balance looks like a sash pulley but has a metal tape coming out of it; a spring inside the device provides the tension. If the spring or the metal tape breaks, replacing it is easy, but you may have a hard time finding the part itself.

A head jamb spring has a pair of springs at the top of the window. Two strings lead to the sashes, where they connect via pins. You can access the unit by removing a vinyl cover. Again, replacing it is easy but finding the part may be difficult.

Mending a wood sash

1 To strengthen a wood sash that is coming apart, remove the sash and place it on a flat table. Tighten a bar or pipe clamp and check that the sash is square. Using a long ⅜-inch drill bit, bore two holes so they pierce the tenon.

2 Loosen the clamp, pull the pieces slightly apart, and squirt wood glue into the gap. Tighten the clamp, squirt polyurethane glue or exterior wood glue into the holes, and tap in ⅜-inch dowels. Trim the dowels with a handsaw and sand smooth.

Using mending plates

A quicker though less effective and less attractive solution is to use mending plates. While it is best to remove the sash to tighten the corner joint and square the unit, this repair can be done while the sash is in the window. Hold the plate in place and drill pilot holes, then drive the screws.

WHAT IF...
The sill is rotted?

1 If rot does not extend all the way through a board, you can repair the spot. Chisel away all loose, rotted wood. Drill a series of ¼-inch holes in the wood.

2 Use exterior-grade filler or mix a batch of two-part epoxy filler and press it into the holes. Use a putty knife or a plastic scraper to roughly form the area.

3 Before the filler has fully hardened, use a shaping tool or paint scraper to make the surface nearly smooth. After the filler has dried, finish smoothing with a sanding block.

REPAIRING CASEMENT WINDOWS

Casement windows are usually made of wood or metal. The sash is attached to the frame with a hinge. A cranking mechanism called an operator attaches, via an arm, to a channel on the underside of the sash. Once the sash is closed, a latch grabs it and tightens it against the frame.

If a casement is difficult to operate, the solution is often as simple as cleaning and lubricating the gears in the operator or the other moving metal parts. If metal parts are broken, they must be replaced.

If the operator and lock work fine but the window is difficult to close, you may need to scrape and sand away caked paint. If bare wood is binding, then the sash should be planed to make it fit correctly.

Finding replacement parts can be difficult. If you can find the make and model of the unit, you may be able to contact the manufacturer or an online parts supply source to obtain the parts you need.

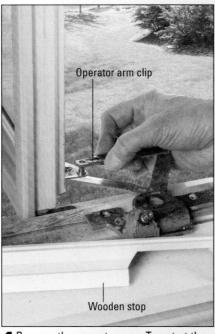

Operator arm clip

Wooden stop

1 Remove the operator arm. To get at the arm, you may need to pry off a wooden stop. The operator arm shown disengages by means of a clip. Other types require you to slide the operator arm along the channel until it reaches the access slot. Then you push the arm down and pull it out.

2 Wire-brush away any rust and clean the arm with mineral spirits or other solvent. Apply lubricant to the joints.

PRESTART CHECKLIST

☐ **TIME**
1 or 2 hours for most repairs

☐ **TOOLS**
Screwdriver, wire brush

☐ **SKILLS**
Minor mechanical skills

☐ **PREP**
Place a drop cloth on the floor near the window.

☐ **MATERIALS**
Replacement parts as needed, grease or spray lubricant, cloths for cleaning, an old toothbrush

WHAT IF...
The arm runs on a track?

The operator arm of some casements runs in a track that can clog with dirt and debris. Clean the track on the underside of the sash with a wire brush, then wipe with a solvent-soaked rag.

STANLEY PRO TIP

Replace a handle

If a handle spins without opening the window, splines in the handle or on the operator shaft have been stripped. Buy a replacement crank that is adjustable to fit a variety of spindles. Slip on the correct ring, add the handle, and tighten the setscrew.

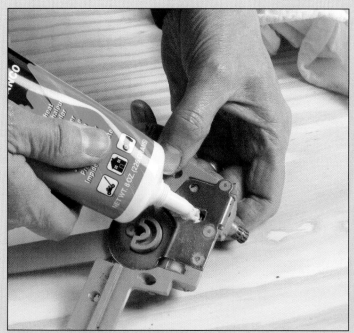

3 Clean the gears with solvent and a toothbrush, then wipe with a rag. Slowly turn the crank to see that the gears mesh. If you see broken parts, replace the operator. Otherwise, apply grease, replace the cover, and test.

4 If the crank assembly still won't work, remove the mounting screws, slide it out, and buy an exact replacement.

WHAT IF...
An awning window needs repair?

An awning window may have an operator at the side or at the bottom center of the window. Either way, the operator mechanism is similar to that of a casement window.

If its operation is not smooth, remove the arm, which may be connected by means of a clip or two on the underside or side of the sash. Clean and lubricate the arm.

Awning arms sometimes get bent. If you cannot straighten the arm using pliers, you may need to replace the operator.

To clean the operator arm on an awning window, begin by removing its cover (if necessary) and unfastening the mechanism from the sash.

Service the operator as you would a casement window: Remove the cover, clean, and lubricate. To remove an operator, straighten the arms and pull them through.

STANLEY PRO TIP

Locate where it binds

A casement window that binds even a little will be difficult to operate. Watch closely while slowly closing the window and mark any spots that bind. If you place a piece of paper covered with soft pencil marks (or carbon paper, if you can find it) between the sash and frame and then close the window, the binding spots will be revealed as dark smudges.

REPAIRING SLIDING WINDOWS

Most sliding (also called gliding) windows have one or more sashes that slide along metal tracks at the bottom and top of the frame. Sometimes the tracks are wood or vinyl. Sashes may have nylon rollers on the bottom and sometimes the top as well.

The most common problem is a dirty bottom track. The solution is to clean and lubricate the track. The rollers on the bottom of the sash can pick up dust and may need to be cleaned as well.

A catch, which secures the window when closed, can fail. You may be able to bend a small part to make it work, but often the solution is to replace the catch.

Finding replacement parts can be difficult. If you can find the make and model of the unit, you may be able to contact the manufacturer or an online parts supply source to obtain the parts you need.

PRESTART CHECKLIST

☐ **TIME**
1 or 2 hours for most repairs

☐ **TOOLS**
Screwdriver, pliers, hammer, wire brush, vacuum, putty knife

☐ **SKILLS**
No special skills needed

☐ **PREP**
Place a drop cloth on the floor near the window.

☐ **MATERIALS**
Replacement rollers (glides) or latch as needed, spray graphite lubricant

Fixing a rough-gliding slider

1 To remove a sliding sash, remove any security devices that may be holding it in place. Lift the sash into the top track, tilt the bottom out, and remove the window. With some models you need to align the rollers with notches in the bottom track before the sash will tilt out.

2 Vacuum the track, then clean with a solvent-dampened rag. Continue to clean until all the debris is removed.

WHAT IF...
The track is bent?

To straighten a bent track, place a piece of hardwood against it and tap with a hammer. If that doesn't work you can try using pliers, but work carefully so you don't create a series of small kinks.

WHAT IF...
The latch is not catching?

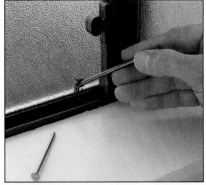

If a latch doesn't grab, first check for an obstruction in the tracks that may keep the sash from closing fully. Inspect the weatherstripping, which can wad up and make closing difficult. You may be able to adjust the latch by loosening a screw, moving the latch, and retightening the screw. If it still doesn't work, replace it.

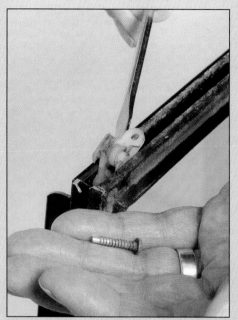

3 If the bottom roller (or glide) does not roll, try cleaning it. If it still does not operate, remove it. On a wood sash you can unscrew the roller unit and remove it. For some metal units you may have to first disassemble the bottom rail. Knock the pieces apart using a hammer and a block of wood.

4 Slip a new roller unit in and tighten the mounting screws. If you had to dismantle the window, reinstall the bottom rail.

5 When replacing the window it often helps to ease the rollers over the lip of the track with a putty knife.

Solve a rattling window

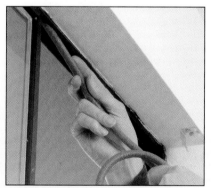

For quick repair to seal the unit for the winter, push tubular insulation into the channels. If you can find replacement insulation for your type of window, remove the old one and clean the surface with a solvent-soaked rag. Use a slightly thicker insulation if needed to create a good seal. Replace the cover, reinstall the sliding sash, and test.

STANLEY PRO TIP: **Burglarproofing**

A security bar firmly secures a sliding window so it can't be opened from the outside. Some models swing down to secure the sash (above) and can be adjusted to allow a slight opening for ventilation. Quick-open security clips (above) allow you to open a sliding window with relative ease. Page 67 shows other security options for sliding windows.

SCREEN AND STORM WINDOW REPAIRS

Storm and screen windows made with wood frames may seem old-fashioned, but they can last many decades and seal effectively if properly maintained. To add weatherstripping that can make wood storms serious protection against cold-air infiltration, see page 62.

Repair rotted wood with two-part epoxy filler, as shown on page 43. Missing or broken pieces of screen mold are easy to replace. You may not be able to find an exact match for old screen mold, but you can probably find a pretty close substitute.

Metal storm and screen windows are frequent troublemakers, partly because they are often of poor quality and may have been hastily installed. You can sometimes—but not always—purchase replacement parts; manufacturers are often regional and may be out of business. For a tighter seal consider installing better-quality storms, as shown on page 69.

PRESTART CHECKLIST

☐ **TIME**
  1 or 2 hours to make most repairs

☐ **TOOLS**
  Hammer, tape measure, putty knife, tin snips, chisel, flat pry bar, drill, pliers, stapler, spline roller

☐ **SKILLS**
  General carpentry skills

☐ **PREP**
  Remove and inspect storm sashes. Contact manufacturers for parts as needed.

☐ **MATERIALS**
  Screening and glass as needed, exterior wood glue or polyurethane glue, dowels, finish nails

Replacing screening in a wood frame

1 Use a putty knife, then a flat pry bar to remove the screen molding. If you work carefully you can often do this without breaking the molding.

2 Place the window on a table or a pair of sawhorses with 2×4s across them. Slip 2×2s under each end and clamp or weigh down the middle so the frame is bowed.

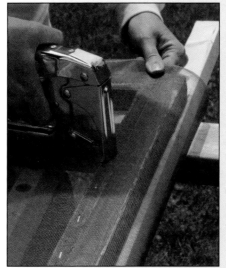

3 Use tin snips to cut screening about 2 inches wider and longer than the frame. Place the piece on top of the frame. Working from the center toward the ends, staple the screening to the wood, pulling it taut as you go.

4 Remove the clamps or weights. When the frame straightens, the screening will be pulled taut. Replace the screen molding or install new molding. Drive nails through new holes or drive larger nails through the old holes. Trim excess screen.

Replacing screening in a metal frame

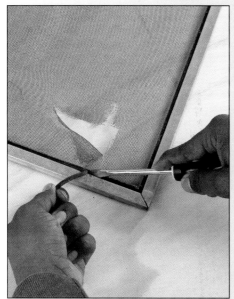

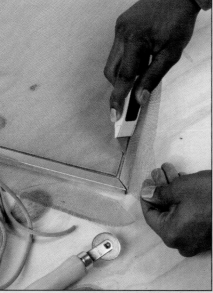

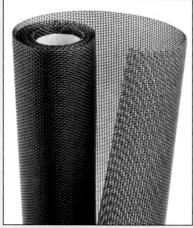

1 Use a straight (regular) screwdriver to pry the vinyl spline up at a corner. Pull the spline out with your fingers. If the spline is in good shape and you pull carefully so it doesn't stretch, you can reuse the old spline. Otherwise buy new spline material. Cut a piece of screening several inches larger than the frame.

2 Have a helper hold the screening at one end while you pull it taut and and use the convex side of a spline roller to press the screen into a groove. Then use the concave side to push the spline into the frame. Cut the spline with a utility knife when you get to the end of a line. Trim excess screen.

Use standard vinyl or aluminum screening for most applications. Pet-proof screening is strong enough to withstand scratching claws. For a room that overheats from the sun, install sun-shading screening, which is, predictably, somewhat dark.

WHAT IF...
You need to strengthen a wood frame?

If a wood storm or screen frame is coming apart at a corner, first repair rotted sections (see page 43). Secure the joint with a long bar clamp or a pipe clamp to make sure it will go back together tightly; you may need to scrape out debris and

built-up paint. Pull the joint apart slightly and squirt polyurethane glue onto both sides of the joint tongue.

Drill two ⅜-inch holes through the joint. Squirt a little glue into the holes, then tap ⅜-inch

dowels into the holes. After the glue dries, trim the dowels flush to the frame with a handsaw, then sand smooth.

Replacing a corner joint

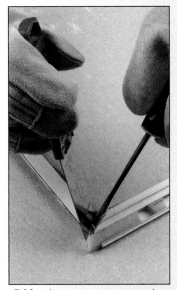

1 Metal storm or screen sashes often loosen at the corners. Many joints simply pry apart; if needed use a putty knife to work the joint open. With some joints the fasteners may be held with a screw. Others are held with a crimp or two in the frame that you will have to drill out.

2 Pry the joint completely open by twisting with a screwdriver. You may have to tap outward on the joint with a hammer to pull the corner apart.

3 Push the old corner fasteners out of the frame with a screwdriver. Take parts to a home center or hardware store to find matching components. Failing that, try looking online.

4 Push or tap the replacement fitting in. Replace any screws. Re-create a crimp with a hammer and a nail set.

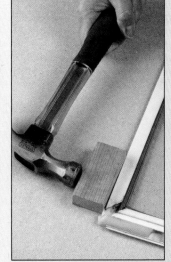

5 Slip the gasket over the edges of the glass and gently push the frame onto the glass and gasket.

6 Push the frame pieces together. Tap lightly with a hammer if necessary. Drive in any retaining screws.

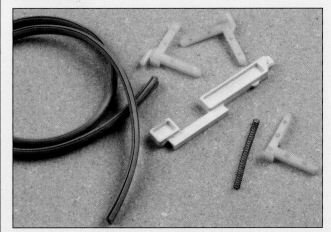

STANLEY PRO TIP: **Fragile parts**

Storm windows have a number of small plastic and metal parts that are easily broken. In addition to corner keys, you may need to replace sliding locks, sash hangers, and pull tabs. The weatherstripping often compresses or comes out; use a spline roller to replace it with new weatherstripping. If the sash is bent and you need to make a new one, see opposite page.

Replacing glass in a metal storm window

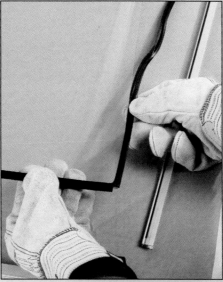

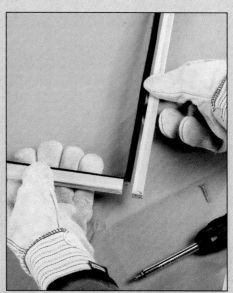

1 If the broken pane has large pieces that will not pull out easily, disassemble the frame in order to remove the glass. Unscrew the retaining screws and remove at least one piece of framing.

2 Order a new pane the same size and thickness as the old. Unless the rubber gasket is in great shape, buy new gasket material as well. Slip the gasket onto the edges of the pane. At the corners, make a cut in the gasket so it wraps the glass without stretching or bulging.

3 Slip the pane and gasket into the frame's groove; make sure it seats firmly at all points. Push on the frame piece that you removed, check that all the corners are tight, and drive the retaining screws.

Making a new metal screen sash

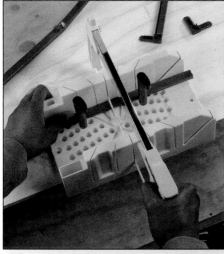

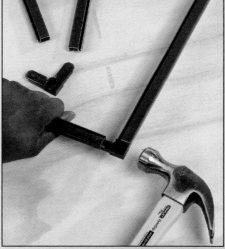

1 Buy a screen frame kit from a hardware store or home center. Use a hacksaw to cut the pieces to length, taking into account the width of the plastic corner pieces.

2 Assemble the frame by slipping the corner pieces into one piece, then sliding the next piece onto the corner piece.

3 Install screening using a spline roller, as shown on page 49.

REPLACING WINDOWSILLS

A windowsill is the part that extends outside the house; what is commonly called an interior sill is technically the stool. A wood sill is one of the few exterior surfaces that presents a horizontal face to the elements, making it vulnerable to rot.

Check the extent of rot by poking with a screwdriver; where you can easily push in, the wood is rotted. If the sill is rotted near the exterior casing, the casing may be rotted as well. If the sill is rotted all the way through, the house's framing or siding may be rotted as well.

If the rot is localized, use wood hardener and two-part epoxy filler to repair it (see page 43). Replacing a sill is tricky but only requires basic carpentry skills. If the old sill is so rotted that you cannot use it as a template, measuring and cutting will be more difficult.

Buy special sill stock or cut the sill out of 2×6 (1½×5½ inches). If the sill is 1 inch thick, use ⁵⁄₄ decking or buy special sill stock. Use pressure-treated lumber to resist rot.

PRESTART CHECKLIST

☐ **TIME**
About half a day to remove an old sill and replace it

☐ **TOOLS**
Tape measure, hammer, flat pry bar, circular saw or power mitersaw, handsaw, small hacksaw, large slip-joint pliers, reciprocating saw, drill

☐ **SKILLS**
Basic carpentry skills

☐ **PREP**
Spread a drop cloth on the floor near the window and protect the plants outside. Set up a pair of sawhorses.

☐ **MATERIALS**
Lumber to match the sill in thickness and width (it's OK if it's wider), shims, galvanized nails or decking screws, primer and paint

1 Start by removing the stool. You may need to remove the interior casing molding first. Some stools are rabbeted and overlap the sill. Others are straight and simply butt up against the sill. To remove a rabbeted stool, pry it up from the outside. Pry out a straight stool from the inside.

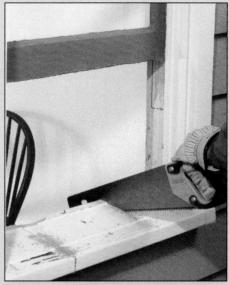

2 If the sill is so rotted you will not be able to use it as a template (step 4), measure its thickness, width, inside length, and outside length or make a cardboard template. Use a handsaw or reciprocating saw to cut through the sill in two places (to produce three pieces).

STANLEY PRO TIP

Protecting a window from rot

A sill should be angled slightly down and away from the house so water can run off easily. If there are places where water can collect, fill them with wood epoxy or caulk so water can flow away easily.

Keep the sill coated with paint. When you notice bare spots, prime and paint them.

6 Push the new sill into the jamb grooves on each side. If you need to tap it into place, use a piece of scrap lumber to protect the sill. If needed, insert shims under the sill so it rests firmly on framing. If the stool is straight, you will need to shim it as well.

3 Use a flat pry bar to pry out the middle piece and then the side pieces. You may need to use a reciprocating saw or small hacksaw to cut through the nails that poke through the jambs on each side. Or use slip-joint pliers to pull them out.

4 Place the three pieces on top of the new lumber and mark the new piece for cutting. The sill is likely beveled at the outside edge. If you buy sill stock, this bevel will already be cut. Otherwise cut it with a circular saw or tablesaw.

5 Cut the sill to length and start the notches with a circular saw or power mitersaw. Finish the notch cuts with a handsaw or reciprocating saw.

7 Attach the sill by driving screws up and into the jambs. Push in shims as needed to make the sill firm at all points.

8 Angle-drive nails from the top and into framing below. If possible do this only where the nails will be covered by the molding. Replace the apron and the casing.

9 After all the trim is installed, apply exterior caulking to the joints. Prime and paint the sill.

WINDOW UPGRADES

Once your windows are in good working order (see Chapter 2), make sure they look good and are equipped to keep out the elements. This chapter shows how to upgrade your windows so they are as good as—or even better than—new.

Painting the exterior

A new coat of paint on your window boosts its appearance and prolongs its life. First repair the glazing putty as needed and wait for the putty to dry. Use an angled sash brush to apply high-quality exterior paint or solid stain, following the techniques shown on pages 56–57.

Tightening up

You can change a drafty old window into an energy-efficient unit by first installing weatherstripping and then upgrading your old storm windows or installing new storms. These are labor-intensive projects, but they can save you plenty compared with the cost of having new windows installed.

As a prelude to weatherstripping, you will likely need to make repairs to the window so it operates smoothly (pages 34–47). Choose types of weatherstripping that will seal well and are long-lasting; we'll show you the most popular options.

Storm windows need not be the flimsy, cheap-looking units that are so common. Old wood storms can be made more efficient, or you can install high-quality new storms that will earn back their extra cost in a few years of energy savings.

Window hardware is inexpensive and easy to install. It can improve your home's security and upgrade the look of a room to boot.

Small improvements make a big difference in windows.

CHAPTER PREVIEW

Painting a window
page 56

Weatherstripping windows
page 58

Upgrading wood storm windows
page 62

Window hardware and glass upgrades
page 64

Storm windows aren't created equal
While storm windows are not difficult to install, adding them to your house is a considerable investment. See page 69 for tips on what to look for when you shop for storm windows.

Installing storm windows yourself is a straightforward job that will reward you with draft-free windows in the winter and easy changeover to screens in the summer. Only a basic tool kit is required.

Making windows more secure
page 66

Installing new storm windows
page 68

PAINTING A WINDOW

Many people think of painting as something anyone can do. But don't take the job lightly—painting mistakes can cause plenty of window problems. Take the time to learn how to do the job right.

Preparation is vital. New windows should be sanded and primed. If the surface of an old window is rough because of paint buildup or other causes, new paint will not correct the situation. Scrape and sand as needed until the surface looks and feels smooth.

A coat of paint may hinder the window from closing easily. See pages 38–39 for tips on how to improve operation. Before painting, scrape or sand until the window works well, then sand some more to allow for the new paint's thickness.

To make sure the new paint will stick, sand all surfaces first. (A coat of primer will also ensure stickability, but the extra paint thickness can pose problems on an old window.) Whenever you apply paint you will create a slight ridge. To ensure a smooth surface, aim to always maintain a wet edge.

PRESTART CHECKLIST

☐ **TIME**
About 2 hours to lightly sand and paint a medium-size window; more time if extensive sanding is needed

☐ **TOOLS**
High-quality paintbrush (a 2- or 2½-inch tapered brush is useful), solid and foam sanding blocks, paint scrapers, straight razor blades, razor-blade scraper, putty knife

☐ **SKILLS**
Painting is a skill that you can learn in a couple of hours if you work carefully.

☐ **PREP**
Protect the floor with drop cloths. For high windows use a stable ladder.

☐ **MATERIALS**
Sandpaper, wood filler, paint, primer

1 Sand all the surfaces smooth. When sanding molding profiles use a foam sanding block or a loose piece of sandpaper. If you have heavy paint buildup, scrape first with a pull-type paint scraper or use a heat gun or chemicals to strip the paint.

2 Start near the glass. Load the brush on one side only and hold the full width of the bristles against the wood as you work. Lap the paint slightly onto the glass.

WHAT IF...
You need to fill holes?

Individual holes in wood can be filled and smoothed successfully. If you have areas that are rough, using wood filler (or putty) can improve the surface, but it will be difficult to make it look perfectly smooth.

Use a taping knife or putty knife to spread wood filler or wood spackle over the area.

Press in to make sure it sticks, then mound it up just a bit so you can sand it down later.

Once the filler has hardened, smooth the area using a solid sanding block. Use a foam sanding block or loose sheet of sandpaper only if the area is not flat. The area should look and feel smooth.

3 While the paint is still wet, press a straight razor blade flat against the glass and scrape alongside the wood (but not tight against the wood). This will make a straight paint line and will force the paint to seal the joint between the wood and the glass.

4 Working to maintain a wet edge, paint the sides of the sashes next. Finish with long, slow strokes to produce a smooth surface.

5 Do not force paint into the crack between a moveable sash and the frame, or it will be difficult to move the sash. Periodically move the sashes up and down to make sure they are not painted shut. Use a putty knife rather than your fingers to avoid marring the paint job.

STANLEY PRO TIP

Remove the sash first

If it is convenient, remove the sashes for painting. To ensure smooth operation take care not to paint the sides of the sashes.

STANLEY PRO TIP

Painting a vinyl or metal window

A metal or a colored vinyl window can usually be painted successfully. To be sure the paint will stick, sand first. For the best adherance apply oil-base or 100 percent acrylic paint.

A white vinyl window may not hold paint well. Sand the window thoroughly, then apply a coat of alcohol-base primer (also called white shellac) followed by a coat of 100 percent acrylic or oil-base paint. The paint will probably require touching up every few years.

WHAT IF...
You use masking tape?

Some people prefer to use masking tape. Apply the tape in a straight line about 1/8 inch from the wood (so the paint laps onto the glass slightly). Pull off the tape while the paint is still wet.

WEATHERSTRIPPING WINDOWS

Most heat loss at a window occurs through gaps between the sashes and the frame. Even small gaps can be big energy-wasters. On a windy day hold a piece of tissue paper or plastic wrap near the window and move it around. Wherever you see movement (either outward or inward), there is a significant leak.

The first step is to caulk, especially on the exterior, although some interior caulking is helpful as well. Also check that the glazing putty on the outside is free of gaps and seals tightly against the window. Where glazing is failing scrape it out and apply new glazing (see page 61). On the inside see that the joint between the glass and the sash is sealed with paint (see pages 56–57).

Weatherstripping where two surfaces push together (the horizontals of a double-hung window and the verticals of a casement or sliding window) is straightforward. Where two surfaces slide against each other (the verticals of a double-hung window and the horizontals of a casement or slider) calls for more precision.

Nail-on tubular gasket

Spring bronze

V-strip

Self-stick foam

Rope caulk

Self-stick tubular gasket

Nail-on weatherstripping is the most durable choice if you have a wood window. Spring bronze works well for gaps that are consistent in width. It is also the best looking product. Where the gap is large and uneven and looks are not as important, tubular vinyl is a good choice. Strips of felt (not shown) are a poor choice because they don't seal well and are not durable.

Self-stick weatherstripping is easy to cut, making it the most convenient choice. If you are choosing self-stick V-strip tape, be sure it is made of EPDM (ethylene-propylene-diene-monomer), which stays flexible for many years, even when exposed to extremely low temperatures.

Foam weatherstripping is easy to apply and fills large and uneven gaps effectively. However it usually doesn't last long. Open-cell foam is the best at bouncing back after being compressed, but it can only be used on the inside. Closed-cell foam is weather resistant but short-lived.

For quick but temporary sealing, use rope caulk, which can be removed when the weather gets warm.

PRESTART CHECKLIST

☐ **TIME**
1 or 2 hours to apply weatherstripping to all the moving parts of a double-hung window

☐ **TOOLS**
Tape measure, tin snips, scissors, caulk gun, hammer, drill

☐ **SKILLS**
Measuring, cutting with tin snips, driving small nails

☐ **PREP**
Determine where your window needs weatherstripping (see right).

☐ **MATERIALS**
Weatherstripping, brads, caulk, spray foam insulation, fiberglass insulation, rags and perhaps mineral spirits

Where windows lose it

A double-hung window has a number of potential leak points. Most prominent are where the bottom of the upper sash meets the top of the lower sash, where the sashes slide against the jamb, and where the bottom sash meets the stool. These gaps must be sealed with weatherstripping.

Gaps can also be found on the outside of the casing, the underside of the stool, and the apron. To seal them, paint and caulk.

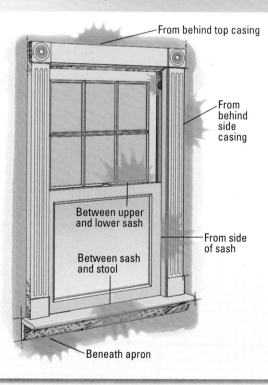

From behind top casing

From behind side casing

Between upper and lower sash

From side of sash

Between sash and stool

Beneath apron

Caulking

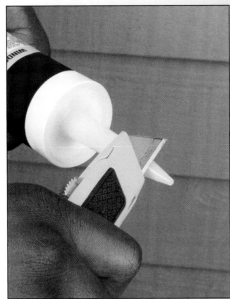

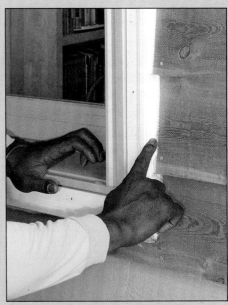

1 Cut a caulk tube's tip using a sharp utility knife; a straight, clean cut contributes to a smooth caulk line. Some people prefer to cut at a steep angle, while others prefer a nearly straight cut. Cut nearer the tip for a smaller bead of caulk. With some caulk tubes you must also poke a wire or long nail through the tip to break a seal.

2 It takes a bit of experience to produce a smooth bead of caulk, so start caulking in an inconspicuous location. Get in a comfortable position and rest the tip against the joint. Squeeze the trigger until caulk emerges, then continue to squeeze as you move the tip along the joint.

3 If the bead looks good, leave it alone. Otherwise use your finger to tool it; this tends to smear the caulk, but it does ensure sticking on both sides of the bead.

(pages 74–79)

WHAT IF...
Counterweight openings need to be insulated?

If you have installed a replacement window or replacement sashes (pages 74–79), the cavity for the sash weights can be filled with insulation. Fill the opening by gently stuffing

with fiberglass insulation. Or fill the spaces with spray foam (the nonexpanding type is easiest to control).

STANLEY PRO TIP

Rope caulk: a seasonal fix

For an added measure of weatherstripping during cold months, unroll and press in rope caulk where the sash meets the stops, between the top of the lower sash and the bottom of the upper sash, and in the pulley. The window cannot be opened while the caulk is in place, so remove it in the spring.

Sealing the top or bottom

Test to be sure you will be able to close the window before you apply thick weatherstripping to the underside or top of a sash. To apply self-stick foam, first make sure the surface is clean and dry. Cut the foam with scissors or tin snips. Peel off the backing and press the foam into place.

Cut spring bronze with tin snips to fit precisely. Taking care not to bend the metal as you work, hold the piece in place and drive the little bronze nails. Drive two or three nails, test to be sure the window will close, then drive the rest of the nails.

Tubular vinyl can seal large cracks, though it does detract from the appearance of a window. Cut the strips with scissors. Close the window and press the vinyl firmly into place while you drive the small nails.

WHAT IF...
You must seal a pulley?

Cold winter air can come in through the pulley slots. Plastic covers are available or you can press in removable rope caulk (see page 59) to fill the gaps. Or simply cover with duct tape. Remove the caulk or tape before opening the window in the spring.

STANLEY PRO TIP: **Plastic shrink wrap**

To seal a window for the winter season only, purchase a shrink-wrap window cover kit. Apply the double-sided tape all around the casing, then carefully apply the plastic to the tape. Use a blow dryer to shrink the plastic and make it taut.

Sealing the sides

To install spring bronze along the sides of a lower sash, raise the sash all the way up. Cut the bronze to the height of the sash. Slip it up the sash as far as needed, nail in place, then close the sash to test.

For a casement or sliding window, apply V-strip to the side of the sash or jamb for a good seal. Make sure the surface is clean and dry. Cut the V-strip to fit and hold it in position. Peel back the paper as you press the self-stick strip in place.

Self-adhesive foam also works well for a casement or sliding window. The foam comes in various thicknesses; test to be sure the window will close after you apply it.

Window well covers

Measure a basement window well and purchase a cover that will fit. Attach with screws and caulk the edges.

Repair glazing putty if it is cracked, missing in spots, or curling from the glass. Use a putty knife or chisel to scrape away loose putty. Clean the area, apply a little linseed oil, and apply putty as shown on pages 34–37.

Apply caulk around all exterior window molding. Also caulk the inside of the molding and under the sill.

UPGRADING WOOD STORM WINDOWS

Many older storm windows are more picturesque than effective. But don't give up on them, especially if you like the way they look. In addition to the repairs shown on pages 48–51, you can add hardware and weatherstripping that will make them seal more effectively.

Often you will find built-up and perhaps peeling paint on the old wood storms and the frames or exterior moldings into which they fit. You may need to scrape away several coats of the old paint before you apply new paint.

Building a new wood storm calls for woodworking skills. If you are unable to duplicate the joints you see in the old storms, contact a local woodworker or lumberyard, who may be able to build them. However the cost can be high; it may be time to consider new storm windows (pages 68–71).

PRESTART CHECKLIST

☐ **TIME**
Less than an hour for most repairs

☐ **TOOLS**
Paint scraper, caulk tube, hammer, drill, pliers, screwdriver, plane or sureform tool

☐ **SKILLS**
Using basic carpentry tools

☐ **PREP**
Set the storm in the frame and carefully check for gaps.

☐ **MATERIALS**
Caulk, glazing putty, nails, hardware as needed

A rattling storm window sometimes just needs new closing hardware. An old turn button that is inoperable or caked with paint can be quickly replaced.

Reapply glazing putty to a storm window using a caulk-tube applicator. Or press in a rope of standard putty and smooth it as shown on page 36.

 PRO TIP

Storing storm windows

Clearly mark your windows with their locations. Store them leaning against each other tightly so they will not warp.

WHAT IF...
Your storm window has clips?

Clips can become rusty, paint-encrusted, or just plain worn out. Consider replacing them with new clips or, if replacements are not available, turn buttons.

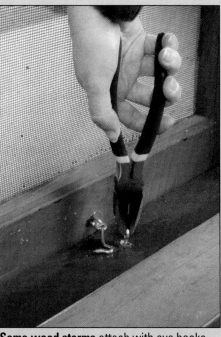

A defective hanging latch can make it difficult for a wood storm to seat properly. If you cannot find a replacement latch at a home center or hardware store, check online sources.

Some wood storms attach with eye hooks on the inside. These must be installed with some precision so they pull the window just tight enough. To install a new one, first install the hook. Slip the hook onto the eyelet, pull the storm tight, and mark for the eyelet's position. Drill a pilot hole and screw in the eyelet.

If a storm is too tight even after the paint has been stripped, use a plane or shaping tool to shave off the excess. See page 127 for tips on planing. Remove enough so the window fits snugly, then remove some more to allow for the paint's thickness. Then paint.

Apply self-stick foam to the surface that faces the storm for a tighter seal. See pages 58–61 for instructions on installing weatherstripping.

If there is room on the sides, you can install V-strip to the sides of the opening.

Condensation buildup between the storm and the window indicates the storm is sealing well. To relieve the condensation, drill two or more ⅜-inch holes, angled upward, into the storm window's bottom rail.

WINDOW HARDWARE AND GLASS UPGRADES

Installation of the upgrades on these pages is usually quick and easy, but don't take the job lightly. If a handle or lock is installed out of alignment, it is often difficult to move a screw that crucial $1/8$ or $1/4$ inch to ensure proper engagement. That may mean having to fill screw holes with wood putty followed by sanding and even a bit of touch-up painting.

Brass-plated hardware looks good at first, but it may appear dingy and worn in a few years. Spend a bit more for solid brass or choose nickel or chrome units.

Applying a low-E film to standard window glass will give a window the energy-saving benefits of low-E glass (see page 17). New decorative glass films can dramatically change the appearance of a window and a room for small outlays of money and time.

PRESTART CHECKLIST

☐ **TIME**
Half an hour or less to install most hardware items

☐ **TOOLS**
Tape measure, awl, drill, hammer, screwdriver, utility knife, squeegee

☐ **SKILLS**
Careful measuring, drilling pilot holes precisely

☐ **PREP**
Buy new hardware with screw holes that match up with the old holes, or fill, sand, and paint over the old holes.

☐ **MATERIALS**
Hardware usually comes with all needed screws.

Replacing a sash lock

1 New hardware screws will probably not grab well in the old holes unless you fill the holes. Glue in matchsticks, toothpicks, or slivers of wood cut from shims until the hole is fairly tight. Use a utility knife to cut the inserts flush with the wood.

2 Once the glue is dry, drill pilot holes. Install the piece on the upper sash first. To make sure the lock will draw the sashes tightly together, position the lower sash piece and close it halfway; the sashes should be fairly tight. Drill pilot holes and drive screws.

Decorative hardware options

At hardware stores, home centers, decorative hardware specialty stores, and online sources, you can find a variety of pulls and locks ranging from modern to antique in style.

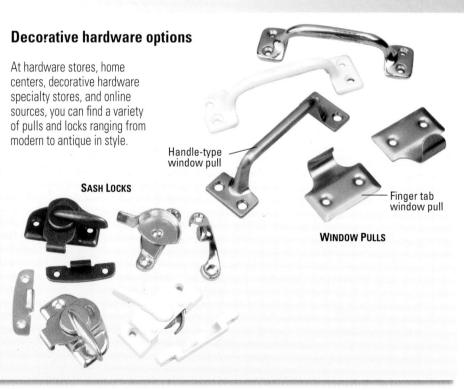

Handle-type window pull

Finger tab window pull

SASH LOCKS

WINDOW PULLS

Applying glass film

1 Clean the window, then spray on water or the wetting solution provided with the film. Apply the film to the window so that it overlaps the glass on all sides.

2 Use your hands to spread the film out, then wipe with a squeegee. Start with a horizontal stroke at the top, then move the squeegee down the middle. Last of all, pull the squeegee down the sides.

3 Once all the bubbles and creases have been removed, cut the edges with a sharp knife. Use a drywall taping knife or an old credit card as a guide to cut a straight line about $1/16$ inch from the frame.

WHAT IF...
You need to replace a pull?

A sash may have one or two pulls, depending on how hard it is to pull up. If you are installing pulls in new locations on the sashes, measure carefully. You can use a cardboard template to make sure you position each pull in the same spot.

STANLEY PRO TIP: **Specialty films**

A new generation of decorative glass films offers a variety of designs, including reflective silver and privacy (shown) as well as stained glass, textures, and even famous artworks.

You can even have a favorite photo turned into a film that you apply to a window. Most films attach via static cling, so they can be easily removed when you want to change the look.

MAKING WINDOWS MORE SECURE

Burglars usually try to enter through a door first, a window second. A thief typically wants to avoid making the noise created by breaking glass. With a good-quality sash lock installed and fastened, the intruder must break a hole in the glass in order to reach a lock that he can turn to open the window. If you want to occasionally keep the window partially open for ventilation, install a wedge lock or bore several holes for a bolt-type lock. If a keyed sash lock is installed, the intruder must break all the glass and crawl through the sash.

With security bars blocking the way, the intruder cannot enter even after breaking the glass. Though some types of security bars are fairly attractive, many people dislike the look.

Another choice is a phone-in security system that notifies the police or security company when one of the sensors placed on windows and doors detects an intrusion.

PRESTART CHECKLIST

☐ **TIME**
Less than an hour for most installations

☐ **TOOLS**
Screwdriver, drill, tape measure

☐ **SKILLS**
Measuring, driving screws

☐ **PREP**
Buy the hardware of your choice. If the screw holes do not match the existing holes in your window, fill and sand the holes.

☐ **MATERIALS**
Screws or bolts are usually included with the hardware.

Locks for double-hung sashes

A hinged wedge lock allows you to open a window partially but keeps the sash from lifting far enough to allow an intruder to enter. Swing it away and you can open the window to any height.

A folding lock for a double-hung window can be unlocked and folded to one side so the sash can be raised.

This device secures the sashes but allows them to be opened with a key. To install, first set the sashes where you want them secured. Drill a shallow hole for a ferrule and a deeper hole for the bolt.

Keyed sash locks are available to fit most double-hung windows. Simply remove the old lock, fill the screw holes (see page 64), drill new fastener holes, and install the unit.

Sliding window

Keyed locks for sliding windows are available in several styles. This type needs no permanent fastening; it simply clips in place before locking.

This inexpensive screw-type lock will secure a sliding window. You simply slip it over the lip of the track, push it against the window, and screw it tight onto the track.

The simplest security measure for a sliding window you want to be able to open periodically is a 1-inch dowel cut to fit between the sliding window and the jamb. Lay it flat in the track to secure the window.

WHAT IF...
You want security bars?

Security bars come in a variety of sizes, each of which is adjustable to suit most any window. Many come with locking mechanisms that permit you to swing the security bars open. They mount on the casing or, for deep-set windows, to the jamb. In each case the fasteners must penetrate to the framing members.

Typically, mounting hardware is provided, often with anchors needed for masonry walls. Center one bracket for the mounting hardware, plumb, drill pilot holes, and attach the fasteners. Use the bars for positioning the opposite bracket. Mounting screws often come with inserts that make the screws difficult to remove.

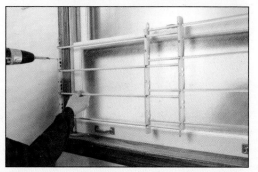

Serious security

Where security is of more concern than seeing the vista outdoors, consider glass block. Prefab units can be ordered that spare you the fuss of mortaring together separate blocks.

INSTALLING NEW STORM WINDOWS

A high-quality storm window can seal out cold air better than a replacement window for a much lower cost. You can install one yourself in far less time than it takes to install a window.

Unfortunately many storm windows are poorly made, with flimsy corners, weatherstripping that doesn't seal well to begin with and soon gets worse, and small parts that easily break. You'll save money in the long run and prevent hassles if you spend more to buy a quality storm.

A standard storm for a double-hung window is triple-track, meaning it holds two glass sashes and one screen, each of which travels on a separate track. If you like to keep the window open in the summer, you can buy a second screen sash to replace the top glass sash.

A storm window is only as good as its installation. The unit must be installed square or the sashes will not slide smoothly. And it must be tightly sealed against the house with caulking and screws.

PRESTART CHECKLIST

☐ **TIME**
Once the unit is purchased, about an hour to install a storm window

☐ **TOOLS**
Framing square, tape measure, drill, paint scraper, caulk gun, hammer, screwdriver, tin snips

☐ **SKILLS**
Measuring and checking for square, applying caulk, driving screws

☐ **PREP**
Choose a quality storm window and order one to fit your opening. Use a stable ladder and protect any plantings below.

☐ **MATERIALS**
Caulk, wood or decking screws (or the screws that come with the storm window)

1 Remove the old storm window or any other hardware that can get in the way of the new storm. To check the window opening for square, first hold a framing square at the corners, then measure the diagonals (see page 76). If the opening is out of square by more than $3/8$ inch, you might be able to adjust the molding to make it square. Otherwise order a storm window that will fit into a smaller opening with square corners.

Measure the horizontal dimension at the top, middle, and bottom of the window, and use the smallest measurement. Also measure the verticals at three points.

HOW TO MEASURE

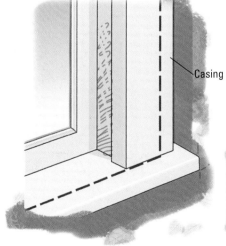
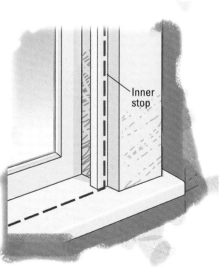

Casing

Inner stop

The storm window is attached to the house by driving screws through a flange. Often you will fasten the flange directly to the casing (above left). When you measure for this type, check that the flange only, not the sash as well, overlaps onto the trim. If your opening has an inner stop (above right) that is at least $1/2$ inch thick, you can fasten the storm to it instead of the trim.

2 Scrape away built-up paint as needed. If you expect to paint in the next few years, consider doing it now; painting will be a bit more difficult after the storm is installed.

3 Set the storm in place in the opening. Have a helper inside check that it is square and that the sashes slide smoothly.

4 If you are installing inside the casing and the stop on the window is narrower than the flange, you can remove the casing or pry it loose so the flange will be behind it. If that is not feasible, cut the flange as necessary, using tin snips.

STANLEY PRO TIP: **Choosing a quality storm**

A high-quality storm window has a frame with tracks that the sashes fit into, much like a double-hung window. (The cheaper type has pins at the sash corners that fit into channels.) The sashes and screen should slide smoothly.

The sashes should lock open securely and be easy to release for closing. The window should feel solid when you grab it at either end and try to twist. (A cheap storm flexes easily.) The tie bar in the middle and the corner joints

should feel solid. The weatherstripping should have a substantial pile that is easy to replace in the future. (A cheap storm has thin, fuzzy weatherstripping that compresses easily and is difficult to replace.)

5 If the flange does not already have screw holes, drill them now. Position them every 8 inches or so.

6 Apply a generous bead of butyl, silicone, or other door and window caulk wherever the window's flange will rest along the sides and top; do not caulk the sill.

WHAT IF...
You want an inside storm window?

If it is not feasible to install an exterior storm window or if it will spoil the appearance of the window, consider interior storms. A typical unit comes as a kit that you can easily build yourself. The pane is usually made of acrylic, and the frame attaches to interior stops using self-stick tape.

9 Once you are certain the window is square, drive the rest of the screws. Scrape away caulk that squeezes out under the flange.

7 Tilt the storm into the opening. Take care to position it correctly the first time so you don't smear the caulk. Press the flanges into the caulk and ensure that the unit is sealed all along the sides and the top.

8 Drive a screw into the center of the top flange and partially drive a screw into the side flanges near the bottom. Test the window's operation. If the sashes are misaligned to the frame, remove the lower screws and adjust the window as needed.

10 A portion of the flange or a flange extender usually must be modified for a tight fit against the sill. Usually you can do this simply by tapping with a hammer and screwdriver to bend the flange.

11 Angle-drive screws to attach the flange or flange extender to the sill on each side.

12 Apply a thick bead of caulk along the flange at the sill. Recaulk other areas as needed. Do not seal the weep holes, which are needed to prevent condensation.

REPLACING WINDOWS

Replacing a worn-out window will enliven your home's appearance, make your rooms more comfortable, and ease heating and cooling costs—all without having to cut any new holes in your walls. Most of these projects can be completed by a fairly handy person (perhaps with a helper) in a day or less. In fact installing a replacement window is sometimes easier than making some window repairs.

Are you a candidate for a replacement window?

Before you buy a replacement window, consider these factors:

■ If the existing window frame is badly out of square, you will need to remove outside and inside trim, as well as the jamb, in order to straighten things. Otherwise the replacement window will appear misaligned—and it may not fit.

■ If your existing jamb, exterior trim, or sill is rotted, cracked, or otherwise damaged, you could make repairs, but it may actually be less work to tear it all out and install a new window, as described in the next chapter, beginning on page 86.

■ Replacement sashes will be the same size as your old sashes, and a replacement window will actually be a little smaller than the old window. If you want to let in more light, consider enlarging the opening in the wall and installing a new window.

Replacement window options

Replacement windows are units designed to be installed into an existing opening. If you have an old wood window, you can likely leave the jambs and molding in place and remove only the sashes. (If you have a metal or vinyl window, you'll have to remove the entire unit.)

A replacement sash kit is the least expensive and simplest installation. However a complete replacement window (also called a pocket window replacement) is not much more difficult or costly. A garden window is the most complicated project and requires that you remove the entire window.

Replacement sashes are, of course, double- or single-hung windows, but replacement windows may be double-hung, single-hung, casement, or sliding. Most of the glass and style options are described on pages 8–17.

Many replacement units have vinyl frames, but you can purchase wood and clad-wood varieties as well. After installing these windows you can reapply the existing interior and exterior trim or install new trim to better match the new window's style.

Complete replacement can be easier than some repairs.

CHAPTER PREVIEW

Installing replacement sashes
page 74

Installing an insert replacement window
page 76

Removing a window
page 80

Installing a garden window
page 82

An old window that needs replacement may provide an opportunity for something bigger and better. If your house has relatively standard window sizes, chances are good you can find a garden window (above) that will fit right in.

INSTALLING REPLACEMENT SASHES

This is a way to make an old drafty window behave like a new, energy-efficient model—without changing its looks in any way. Also called jamb liner kits, replacement sashes are available in wood or vinyl. The liner on either side is vinyl but is barely visible when the sashes are installed.

To buy replacement sashes that fit snugly, measure the width of the window—from jamb to jamb—at the top, middle, and bottom. Use the shortest measurement. For the height, measure from the top jamb to the point where the lower sash meets the sill on the outside. Check that the frame is straight, square, level, and free of twist, following the instructions on page 76.

PRESTART CHECKLIST

☐ **TIME**
About 3 hours to remove old sashes and install replacement sashes with liners

☐ **TOOLS**
Flat pry bar, chisel, framing square, screwdriver, drill, tape measure, angle finder (see step 1), hammer, tin snips

☐ **SKILLS**
Measuring accurately, removing trim pieces, stuffing insulation, caulking, assembling pieces

☐ **PREP**
Follow manufacturer's instructions for measuring and installing.

☐ **MATERIALS**
Replacement sash kit, caulk

1 Use a framing square to make sure the frame is square. It is important that the bottom edge of the bottom sash matches the bevel of the sill. This angle is usually 14 degrees. Use an angle finder, as shown.

2 Remove the inside stops. Use a putty knife or chisel, then a pry bar to remove the stop, holding the lower sash in place.

REPLACEMENT SASH KIT

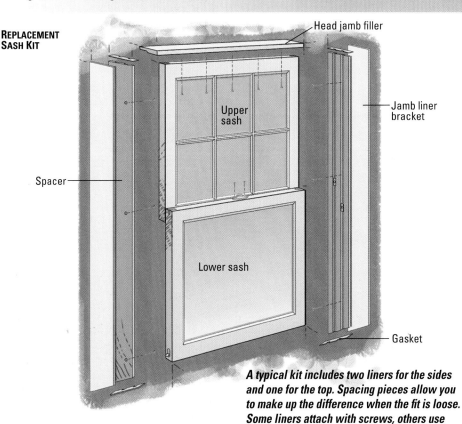

Head jamb filler

Jamb liner bracket

Upper sash

Spacer

Lower sash

Gasket

A typical kit includes two liners for the sides and one for the top. Spacing pieces allow you to make up the difference when the fit is loose. Some liners attach with screws, others use brackets (see steps).

3 Lift the lower sash up and outward. Use tin snips to cut the cord or chain on each side. Remove the screws holding the cord pulleys and pry out the pulleys.

4 Use pliers or a chisel to remove the parting stop (it will not be reused). If painted, score the stop where it meets the jamb before removal. Pull the top sash down, cut its cord or chain, and remove.

5 Install the liner bracket clips as instructed by the manufacturer. Measure to make sure the clips are equidistant from the corresponding clips on the opposite jamb.

6 Snap the liners onto the bracket clips, working from the top down. If the liners do not snap in easily, adjust the clips by carefully bending them with a screwdriver or putty knife.

7 Cut the replacement head parting stop so it is the same size as the width of the upper sash. Press it into place, making sure the weatherstripping faces outward. Fasten it with the finishing nails provided with the kit. Install the filler piece that covers the head jamb.

8 Install the top sash. For a tilt-out sash, slip the sash cam pivots into the liner control slots. Push the bottom into place and test for easy operation and a tight fit all around. Adjust the side jambs as needed and install the bottom sash. Replace the stop molding.

INSTALLING AN INSERT REPLACEMENT WINDOW

A replacement window is made to fit into an existing frame so you don't have to remove the jamb, casing, sill, or exterior trim. Installing one is nearly as simple as installing replacement sashes (pages 74–75). It is, however, important to get the measurement exactly right; err on the side of ordering a replacement smaller than the opening.

These units have for years been called "vinyl replacement windows," but now you can also buy wood and clad-wood models (see opposite page). You'll also find plenty of options for muntins and grilles that offer you the chance to upgrade your windows' style.

Because the insert fits inside the existing window jamb, interior casing and exterior trim may need to be wider than the trim for the old window.

PRESTART CHECKLIST

☐ **TIME**
About 4 hours to remove old sashes and install a replacement window

☐ **TOOLS**
Flat pry bar, chisel, framing square, screwdriver, drill, saw, tape measure, hammer, string, level

☐ **SKILLS**
Measuring accurately, removing trim pieces, stuffing insulation, caulking

☐ **PREP**
Read and follow manufacturer's instructions for measuring and installing.

☐ **MATERIALS**
Replacement window to fit, caulk, shims, finishing nails

1 Check that the window frame (made up of the side and header jambs plus the sill) is square. Hold a framing square against each corner or measure the diagonals. If there is more than a $3/8$-inch difference between the two measurements, check with your window dealer to see if the window will fit. Also check for straightness and twist (below).

2 Measure the distance between the insides of the right and left jambs. Take this measurement in three places: top, middle, and bottom. Also measure from the top of the jamb to the point where the front of the bottom sash touches the sill. Use these measurements to order a replacement window, which should be about $1/4$ inch narrower and shorter than the frame.

STANLEY PRO TIP: **Checking a window frame**

To check a frame for twist, tape two tightly stretched strings at each corner so they cross in the middle, as shown. If there is a gap greater than $1/4$ inch where they meet, the replacement window will not fit well.

Also check the sides for straightness. Hold a level or other straightedge against each side. If at any point you see a gap between the straightedge and the jamb that is greater than $1/4$ inch, the bend will be noticeable when you install the replacement window. You may be able to remove some trim and adjust the jamb so it is straight.

3 Gently remove the inside stops. Pull the bottom sash out of the frame, cut the cords, and remove the sash. Remove the parting stop (as shown) and remove the upper sash (see pages 74–75).

4 Remove the pulleys and the weights, remove the casing, and install insulation in the cavities where the weights were (see page 59). Replace the casing, and caulk to seal it to the wall.

5 Apply a bead of caulk at the joint between the jamb and the sill. Cut a piece of flashing tape (sometimes supplied with the window) 12 inches longer than the opening width and apply it to the sill and partway up the jambs on each side.

STANLEY PRO TIP

Choosing a vinyl replacement window

If you decide to go with a vinyl replacement window, take some time to evaluate the available products. Remove some of the packaging and check for evidence of quality.

■ It's best to buy from a manufacturer that has been in business for a while.

■ The sash locks should feel solid and the sashes should slide smoothly.

■ Welded corners are stronger than corners that are attached with hardware.

■ The thicker the vinyl, the better. A good window will not easily flex when you try to bend it.

WHAT IF...
Vinyl isn't for you?

Once vinyl was the only option for replacement windows, but now you can also choose attractive wood and clad-wood models—or both at once, as shown with the wood interior (left) and clad exterior of this window. Of course vinyl is still the least expensive option.

6 Check the sill for level. If it is not level, place a shim ¹/₂ inch from either of the jambs to achieve level. Attach the shim with a finishing nail.

7 Remove the outer packing from the replacement window, but follow manufacturer's instructions for leaving some of the packing bands and plastic spacers.

8 Pull the sill adapter all the way out. Follow manufacturer's instructions for any other needed adjustments.

Inspecting a window

Inspect each window you buy before installing it. Remove the packing and look for evidence of shipping damage. Open the locking hardware and operate the window by opening and closing the sashes. Each sash should move smoothly. Make sure that all the weatherstripping pieces are in place and that they seal at all points. Watch out for strips that are coming loose or have gaps. When you close the window and lock it, the sash should be completely sealed at all points. Measure the window to ensure that it matches the dimensions you ordered.

12 Slip in shims near the bottom and the middle of each side. Check the frame for square by using a framing square or measuring the diagonals. Slide the sashes up and down, checking that they operate smoothly and align accurately.

13 Cut and remove any remaining packing bands. Check the sides for straightness. You may need to tighten or loosen one or more adjustment screws.

9 Set the window in the frame for a test fitting. Center the window so it fits with about ⅛ inch gap at the sides and the top. Make sure you can drive screws into the frame.

10 Apply a bead of caulk along the outside (blind) stops at the side and head jambs, and where the interior stool meets the exterior sill.

11 Insert the window into the opening. See that it is centered in the frame and press it into the bead of caulk. Near the top on each side, slip in shims and drive mounting screws only partway. (You may have to temporarily remove covers in order to drive mounting screws.)

14 Finish driving the mounting screws near the top. Raise the lower sash, temporarily remove covers if necessary, and drive mounting screws near the bottom.

15 Cut off the shims. Apply a bead of caulk between the window and the side and header jamb. Reinstall the interior stops (which you removed in step 3); the stops will cover the bead of caulk.

16 Install the casing and set the nail heads. Apply the finish of your choice to the interior of the window. You may need to touch up the caulk and the exterior paint.

REMOVING A WINDOW

If your window frame (the jambs and sill) is in bad condition or if you want to change the size of your window, you will need to remove the old window. Chances are you will also end up modifying the siding and changing the wall framing (see pages 26–31 and 88–95).

Unless you don't mind being windowless for a long period, plan the job so you can start framing and installing the new window right away. You can measure for the new window while the old one is in place (page 76). Order and inspect the new window before you remove the old.

You can remove the sashes first (see pages 74–75), then dismantle the frame; this is the best solution for a second- or third-story window. These pages show how to remove the window with the sashes in place.

PRESTART CHECKLIST

☐ **TIME**
About 2 hours to remove a window

☐ **TOOLS**
Hammer, flat pry bar, drill with screwdriver bit, utility knife, slip-joint pliers, reciprocating saw, handsaw

☐ **SKILLS**
Basic carpentry skills

☐ **PREP**
Place drop cloths on the floor and seal off the room's doors with plastic. Place a tarp or sheets of plywood outside the window to protect the lawn and plants.

☐ **MATERIALS**
Protection for interior floors and outside lawn or plants

1 Use a utility knife to slice through any paint or caulk between the interior casing and the wall. Use a flat pry bar and a scrap piece of wood to remove the casing. If you will reuse the casing, use slip-joint pliers to remove the screws (see page 27).

2 If you have an older wood window with sash weights, pull back the cords or chains and cut the ones that attach to the weights for the lower sash. Pull down the upper sash and do the same. Remove the sash weights.

DETACHING WINDOWS FROM THE EXTERIOR

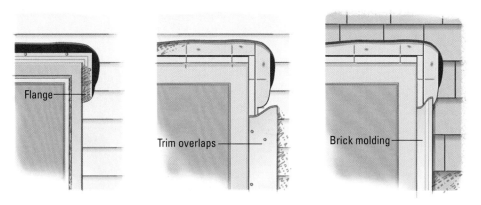

Flange

Trim overlaps

Brick molding

A metal or vinyl window may have a flange that is nailed to the sheathing and covered with siding; in that case you must cut back the siding (see page 83). Molding that rests on top of siding is the easiest to remove. Siding butts up against brick molding.

3 On the exterior cut through any caulk and pry out the molding all around the window. See the illustration on the opposite page for the type of situation you'll encounter. If your window has a flange that is covered by siding, see page 83 for how to cut the siding back.

4 Inside the house pry out the stool (inside sill). It may be easiest to cut through the nails first (see next step). Also remove the apron, which is attached to the wall directly below the stool.

5 Cut through the nails that attach the jamb to the house's framing. A reciprocating saw works best for this, but you can also use a hacksaw. Or slip the notch of a flat pry bar onto the nail's shank and bang hard with a hammer to break the nail.

6 Pull out any insulation and other obstructions, and check that all the nails have been removed. Remove one or both sashes.

7 With a helper standing outside to catch the window, start prying outward. You may need to tap the jambs with a hammer. Once the window is loose and ready to fall, go outside to help pull it out.

INSTALLING A GARDEN WINDOW

Placed in a sunny spot (ideally facing south), a garden window can provide enough sunlight to grow herbs, sprouts, and flowers. Because the window will add extra sunlight to a room, it's usually a good idea to choose a model with low-E glass (see page 17). Some kitchen windows have openable sashes and vents. Most feature water-resistant finishes. Depending on the size of the window and your plants, you may want to have one or two shelves (in addition to the base shelf).

Different windows call for different installation techniques. Most models include a nailing flange or brick molding, requiring that the siding be cut back or removed and reinstalled so it butts against the window or the molding. These pages show installation in an existing window opening, where the siding is kept in place. If you will cut a new hole for the window, see pages 88–95.

PRESTART CHECKLIST

☐ **TIME**
Once the opening has been cut, about four hours to install a garden window; more time may be required if you need to modify the trim on the inside.

☐ **TOOLS**
Tape measure, level, square, hammer, chisel, stapler, utility knife, drill with screwdriver bit, circular saw, handsaw

☐ **SKILLS**
Modifying framing, installing a window, installing window trim

☐ **PREP**
Remove the existing window or cut and frame the opening.

☐ **MATERIALS**
Garden window, shims, roofing felt or building wrap, galvanized roofing nails, casing nails, wood and nails for any additional framing, self-stick flashing tape as required by the manufacturer, caulk, window braces

1 Remove the existing window's casing and perhaps the stool (inside sill) to measure the rough opening. Order a garden window custom-made to fit your opening or plan to modify your framing to accommodate a standard-size unit.

2 Also check the opening to make sure it is square and reasonably straight on its sides. Use a framing square (shown) or measure from corner to corner diagonally (see page 76).

ENSURING A WATERTIGHT SEAL

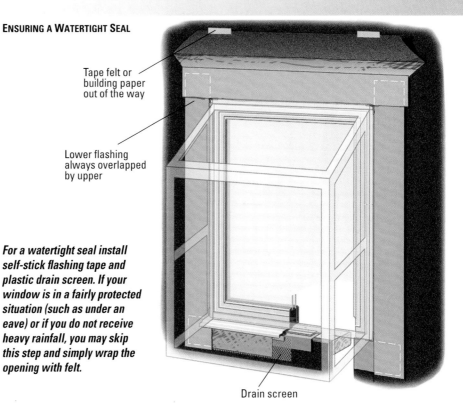

Tape felt or building paper out of the way

Lower flashing always overlapped by upper

For a watertight seal install self-stick flashing tape and plastic drain screen. If your window is in a fairly protected situation (such as under an eave) or if you do not receive heavy rainfall, you may skip this step and simply wrap the opening with felt.

Drain screen

3 Most manufacturers require that the rough opening be ½ inch wider and taller than the window. If you need to make the opening a bit smaller, add pieces of 2× lumber or strips of plywood as needed. Check again for square and straightness.

4 Unbox the garden window and inspect it for flaws. Make sure any operable parts work smoothly and seal tightly. Remove shelves, but keep in place any packing that keeps the unit from warping as you install it.

5 Set the window temporarily in place. Use notched pieces of lumber (inset), set at a slight angle toward the house, to hold the window in place. You may need to tack (partially drive) two nails or screws as well.

6 From the inside check the window for level, plumb, and square, and tap in shims as needed. Note: If you will be installing a continuous support and thick flashing, as shown in steps 9–11, take the thickness of those materials into account when setting the window.

7 On the outside, mark the siding for cutting. If you are adding molding or the window has brick molding, hold it in place and mark.

8 Remove the window. Tack a 1×4 strip as a guide and set the circular saw blade to cut just through the siding or use the method shown on page 29. Cut the lines and finish the cuts using a hammer and chisel. If your window requires it, install a drip cap at the top (see page 98).

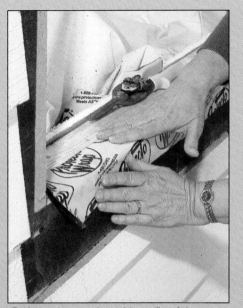

9 Wrap the opening with roofing felt or building wrap. Seal the rough opening as instructed by the manufacturer. For the system shown the first step is to install self-stick flashing to the sill. You may need to spray the area with spray adhesive first.

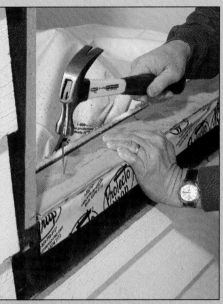

10 Attach the support with nails. This window requires a continuous support, a strip of 1/4-inch plywood slightly shorter than the rough sill.

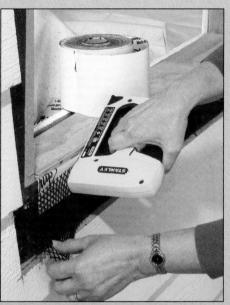

11 Cut a piece of plastic drain screen to the sill length plus 2 inches, center it, and attach with staples. Cut and attach another piece of self-stick flashing over the drain screen.

STANLEY PRO TIP

The right sealants

Caulk is important to ensure your replacement windows are properly sealed. Avoid inexpensive latex-only caulks. A latex/silicone or acrylic/latex caulk has good sealing properties. For the best protection choose silicone caulk formulated to stick well and be paintable (it is often called "Silicone II"). Or choose polyurethane sealer or butyl caulk.

15 Caulk all the joints with high-grade exterior caulk. Paint the new trim soon after installation.

16 While not always required by manufacturers, two metal or decorative wood brackets are good insurance if you have plenty of plants. Locate framing members (don't just attach to the siding) and drive 3-inch screws.

12 Set the window in place, making sure the flange or brick molding rests firmly against the flashing. From the inside adjust with shims as you did in step 6. Drive screws through the flange. If your window does not have a flange, attach through the jambs.

13 Apply self-stick flashing pieces as directed. First install the bottom horizontal, then the sides, then the top piece. (This arrangement ensures that any accumulation of moisture will flow down over the joints and not be able to seep in.)

14 Cut and attach the exterior trim pieces using 8d galvanized casing nails. If fastening brickmold, use 10d galvanized casing nails.

17 Patch drywall as needed. If the window's jamb does not come flush with the interior wall, prepare rip-cut pieces to fit.

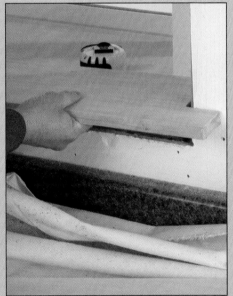

18 Custom-cut a stool (inside sill) if needed. See pages 100–101 for instructions.

19 Cut and install the apron and casing (see pages 101–103) and prep for finishing (see pages 56–57).

Installing New Windows

Installing a new window where there wasn't one before is a major remodeling project. The job is within the abilities of almost any homeowner with good carpentry skills, however.

Start by deciding the style (see pages 8–13) and location of the window. A new window can enhance the appearance of a home's exterior as long as it complements the other windows. Sizing and properly placing windows call for making aesthetic and design decisions as well as some structural determinations. You may benefit by consulting a professional designer.

Framing for a new window
Preparing the opening in the wall for a new window is the toughest part of the job. Actually installing the window—setting the unit in place, shimming it level and plumb, and attaching it to the wall—is a relatively quick and easy job.

An important part of planning is to determine whether wiring, plumbing, or ductwork runs through the new window location. If so you may need to hire a plumber, electrician, or heating expert to move the lines. Sometimes you will need to change the window location.

If the new window is wider than 3 feet, make plans to temporarily support the wall load until you install a header. Otherwise you might seriously damage your home's framing. You will cut through the interior wall surface to expose the framing. Once you have altered the framing to make an opening for the window, you can cut the opening in the outside wall.

Installing the window
Choose a method for sealing the opening that suits your area and take steps to ensure rainwater cannot infiltrate.

Finishing the exterior and interior walls can also take a good deal of time. Consult a book such as *Stanley Interior Walls* for detailed instructions about installing and finishing interior drywall. If you order a simple window with jamb width that matches your wall thickness, it is usually a simple matter to complete the job by adding the casing and other trim. If the fit is not exact, you may need to custom-make trim to fit.

Chapter Preview

Placing windows
page 88

Planning the framing
page 89

Supporting the ceiling
page 90

Framing the opening
page 92

Installing a wood window
page 96

Trimming out a window
page 100

PRO TIP

Comply with local style requirements

Windows can have a dramatic effect on the look of a home. Many areas have rules concerning the styles and even sizes of windows you can install. These rules usually aim to keep all the houses in a neighborhood looking more or less the same—or at least not clashing visually. You may need to bring your plans before a local committee for approval.

Preparing the rough opening is the toughest stage of installing a new window. Setting and squaring up the window itself is straightforward. Also challenging is trimming the interior and exterior. A wide array of basic carpentry tools gets the job done.

Installing a flanged window
page 104

Installing a bay window
page 106

Installing a round window
page 112

Installing a tube skylight
page 114

Installing a skylight
page 116

PLACING WINDOWS

A kitchen window is typically placed higher than the top of a countertop's backsplash—usually 42 inches. In living and dining rooms and perhaps in some bedrooms, you can increase the view by installing windows with the bottom as low as 12 inches above the floor. Placing the bottom of the window about 36 inches above the floor allows wall space to accommodate dressers and other furniture.

For aesthetic and practical reasons (that is, to accommodate the width of a structural header over the window), it's usually a good idea to keep the top of a window at least 16 inches below the ceiling.

In a dining area it is common to have a windowsill at the typical height for a table—about 30 inches.

When possible orient windows to make the best use of natural light and weather.

Weather tends to move from west to east in the United States, and windows placed on east or west walls gain or lose more heat than those facing north or south. A southern exposure will receive plenty of sun, while a northern exposure will receive little direct light. Of course east-facing windows receive morning light and west-facing windows receive sunlight in the afternoon. Consider prevailing winds too.

INDOOR PERSPECTIVE

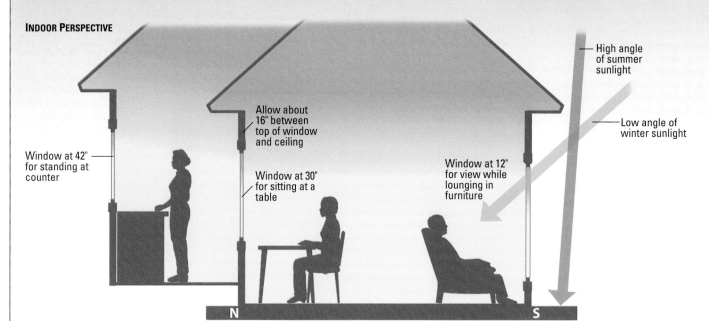

Window at 42" for standing at counter

Allow about 16" between top of window and ceiling

Window at 30" for sitting at a table

Window at 12" for view while lounging in furniture

High angle of summer sunlight

Low angle of winter sunlight

DESIGN OPTION
You have flexibility in the window placement

If you have some latitude on positioning the new window, consider how it will look with the other windows as viewed from the outside. What works well indoors may give the impression from the outside that windows were popped in any old way. Blend the new with the old, even if that means you have to compromise on ideal placement indoors. One technique to meld windows of different sizes (and even styles) is to align the new window along an imaginary horizontal line running from the top of the existing window.

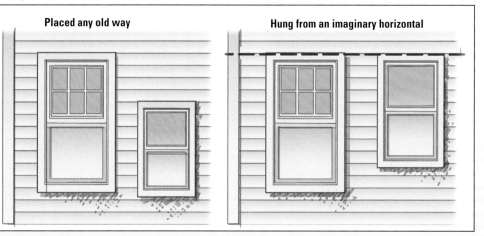

Placed any old way

Hung from an imaginary horizontal

PLANNING THE FRAMING

A window opening has a full-height king stud on each side. Jack studs that reach to the top of the opening are attached to the king studs. A header rests on top of the jack studs. The header is usually made of two pieces of 2× lumber with a piece of ½-inch plywood sandwiched between them; this makes a total thickness of 3½ inches, the same as a 2×4 stud. At the bottom of the opening is a rough sill, which can be made of a single or double thickness of side-laid 2× lumber. Cripple studs support the sill every 16 inches.

When remodeling you may be able to place a small window between two existing studs. You may be able to use an existing stud as a king stud on one side (below center) or you may have to install two new king studs (below right).

WINDOW FRAMING OPTIONS

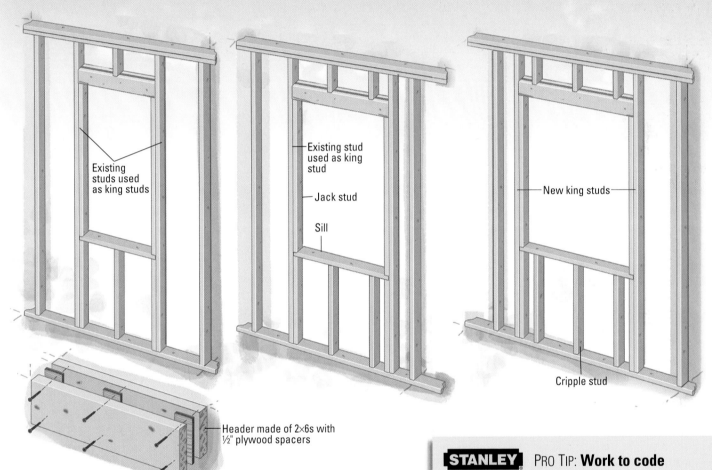

Existing studs used as king studs

Existing stud used as king stud

Jack stud

Sill

New king studs

Cripple stud

Header made of 2×6s with ½" plywood spacers

SUPPORTING THE CEILING

If your new window will be wider than 3 feet, you'll have to remove more than one wall stud. That could cause the wall's top plate—and the ceiling—to sag. If the ceiling joists are perpendicular to the wall and thus rest on the wall frame's top plate (see the illustration below), you must temporarily support the joists. Install the support no farther than 3 feet from the wall.

If the joists run parallel to the wall, supporting them will not help shore up the wall. Use the method shown on the opposite page. Use the same method if your home is built with old balloon framing, which has no top or bottom wall plates.

Build a temporary support that is several feet longer than the new window opening. Buy enough studs so you can place them about 16 inches apart.

PRESTART CHECKLIST

☐ **TIME**
About 2 hours to build a temporary support and wedge it into position

☐ **TOOLS**
Tape measure, hammer, level, circular saw, handsaw, drill with screwdriver bit

☐ **SKILLS**
Basic carpentry skills

☐ **PREP**
Cover the room's floor with a drop cloth. You may choose to remove the drywall or plaster before building the temporary supports.

☐ **MATERIALS**
2×4s, 16d nails or 3-inch screws, shims

1 To determine the direction the joists run through the ceiling, use an electronic stud finder or drill a series of locator holes. This will allow you to plan your temporary support. Then use the stud finder to locate the framing members and plan how you will frame the window (see page 89).

2 Cut out a floor-to-ceiling section of drywall or plaster that is at least 3 inches wider than the desired rough opening. In this case it worked out to cut along one stud; on the other side the cut was made into the cavity between two studs.

TEMPORARY SUPPORT FOR AN EXTERIOR WALL

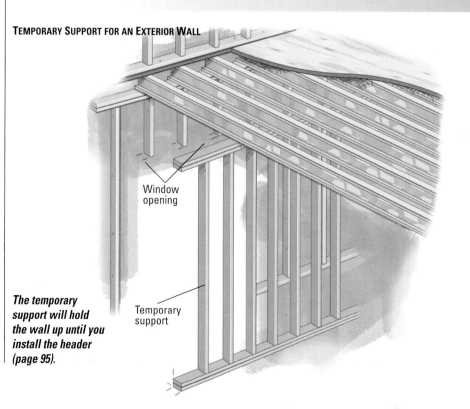

Window opening

Temporary support

The temporary support will hold the wall up until you install the header (page 95).

3 Mark the bottom (sole) plate to indicate where the king studs and jack studs will go. The distance between the jack studs is the width of the rough opening.

4 In the place where you will put the temporary wall, stack three short pieces of 2×4 (for a total thickness of 4½ inches). Measure from the ceiling to the top of the stack. Cut the studs ¼ inch shorter than this measurement.

5 Mark the bottom and top plate for studs every 16 inches. Attach the studs to the plates by driving nails or screws. Add a second top plate. To keep from scraping the ceiling, add a scrap of carpeting to the top plate (see box below). With a helper raise the wall and tap it into place. If the fit is not snug, tap shims under the bottom plate.

WHAT IF…
Joists do not rest on the plate?

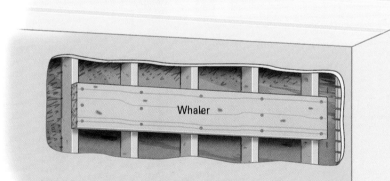

Whaler

If joists are parallel to the wall or if you have a balloon-framed house, remove the drywall or plaster to at least 2 feet above the future opening. Cut a 2×8 whaler to fit across the opening so it attaches to at least one stud on either side that will not be cut. Attach the whaler to the studs with three 3-inch deck or wood screws (not drywall or "all-purpose" screws) driven into each stud.

STANLEY PRO TIP

Protecting the ceiling
A temporary support will likely dent the ceiling. This is especially true if you have a sprayed acoustic (popcorn) ceiling. You can take steps to minimize damage.
■ Make the top piece of the plate out of 2×6 rather than 2×4. This will distribute the weight over a larger area.
■ Attach a strip of carpeting on the top plate to cushion the surface. If you do this be sure to cut the studs shorter by the thickness of the carpet. Staple the carpet in place from the sides, not the top.

FRAMING THE OPENING

When framing for a window in a new location, it is usually easiest to cut an opening in the interior drywall that is quite a bit larger than the window opening. This will require you to patch the walls afterward, but installing framing—especially the header—inside a wall is difficult. If you have plaster walls, you may want to try the surgical method shown on the opposite page.

It is also usually easiest to leave the exterior sheathing and siding in place while you cut the studs and build the framing. This prevents having to replace siding. However if you will be replacing the siding anyway, you can cut a large opening in the exterior at the same time you cut the interior opening. If the window has brick molding or a flange, you will need to cut back the siding to accommodate it (see pages 81 and 83).

See pages 26–31 for general instructions on removing interior and exterior surfaces as well as patching various types of siding. If you have a brick wall, hire a professional mason to cut an opening.

When framing always work carefully to produce a structure that presents a smooth face for the drywall. Install adjoining pieces perfectly flush with each other.

1 You will need at least one new king stud (see the left side of the opening in the illustration below), which is the same length as the other existing studs. Cut two cripple studs; the sill will rest on their tops. (A jack stud will be fastened above so it and the cripple stud sandwich the sill.) Drive a fastener every 12 inches or so, in an alternating pattern.

PRESTART CHECKLIST

☐ **TIME**
A full day to remove interior drywall and frame for a window

☐ **TOOLS**
Tape measure, stud finder, hammer, nail set, flat pry bar, drill with screwdriver bit, level, combination square, framing square, reciprocating saw, handsaw, stapler

☐ **SKILLS**
Measuring, marking, cutting

☐ **PREP**
Place drop cloths on the floor and seal the doorways to prevent dust infiltration. Place a fan in a nearby window and point it outward.

☐ **MATERIALS**
2×4s or 2×6s for framing, shims, 16d and 10d nails or 2- and 3-inch deck or wood screws, plywood, staples

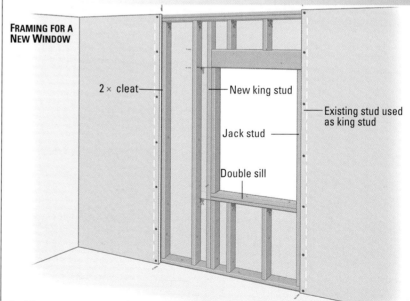

FRAMING FOR A NEW WINDOW

2 × cleat

New king stud

Existing stud used as king stud

Jack stud

Double sill

In this arrangement an existing wall stud is used as a king stud on one side, and a 2×2 or 2×4 cleat is attached to the stud on the other side to provide a nailing surface for patching the drywall after the window is installed. (This is easier and stronger than trying to cut the drywall down the middle of a stud and then using half a stud's thickness for the nailing surface.)

2 Install a king-and-cripple stud combo by wedging the king stud between the top and bottom plates. If framing a cavity push the king-and-cripple stud halfway behind the drywall and drive angled 10d nails or 2-inch screws. (Fastening will probably move the studs over slightly, so start with the studs offset by ¼ inch or so.)

3 If you are using the opposite existing stud as a king stud for your framing, install a 2×4 cripple stud up against it. Tack the jack studs in place, using spacers to stand in for the sill.

4 Mark for the header. Hold a level atop the jack stud and mark across the studs to indicate the bottom of the header. Measure upward to mark where the top of the header will be. Make cutlines about ⅛ inch higher than the measurement. If there is a gap, fill it with shims. Make the bottom cuts (step 7) about ⅛ inch lower than the measurement.

STANLEY PRO TIP: **SURGICAL METHOD**

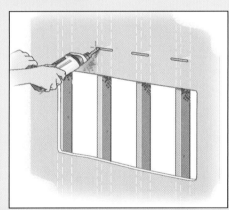

1 If patching walls will be difficult (as when you have plaster walls), you may choose to slip the new framing in. Cut a section of the finished wall that is the correct size of the opening. Use a reciprocating saw to slice through the studs above and below, taking into account the widths of the header and sill.

2 Cut through the studs midway and pull them out. Carefully clean out the openings to allow room for the header and the sill.

3 Slip the new header into the opening and slide in a jack stud at either end to hold the header up. Slip in the sill as well. Angle-drive screws to hold the framing pieces together.

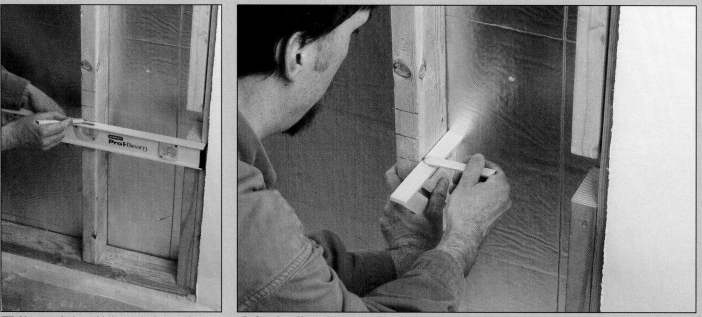

5 Also mark the middle studs for cutting at the bottom. They should be marked for the needed rough opening dimension plus 1½ inches (for a single bottom plate) or 3 inches (for a double bottom plate).

6 Caution: If you have not already done so, install a temporary support for the wall (see pages 90–91) before you start cutting. Complete your marking by using a square to mark across each of the studs to ensure a square cut.

9 To build the header, cut two pieces of 2×6 or 2×8 to the width of the opening plus 3 inches. Cut strips of ½-inch plywood as spacers. Lay the 2×s on top of each other to determine which direction (if any) they "crown," bend upward in the middle. See that their crowns face the same way. Position a spacer every 8 or 10 inches, lay the second 2× on top, and drive two or three 3-inch screws.

10 Set the header on the jack studs with the crown facing up. You may have to hammer it into position. Attach the header with 16d nails or 3-inch screws.

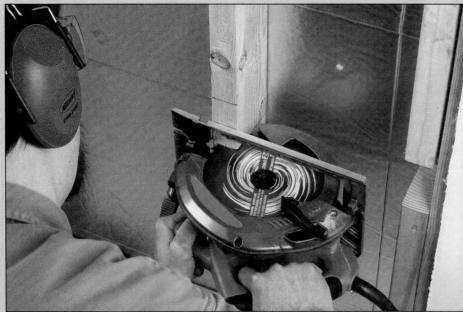

7 Set the blade of a circular saw to full depth, and check to make sure it is square to the saw's baseplate. Cut a scrap piece to confirm that the blade is cutting square. Wearing ear and eye protection, cut the lines with the circular saw.

8 Finish the cuts using a handsaw or a reciprocating saw.

11 Cut one or two pieces to length for the sill. Nail or screw the sill in place. If using two pieces fasten one piece to the top of the cripple studs, then add the second piece.

12 Check the opening for square (see page 76). As long as the opening is ½ inch wider and taller than the window, it is OK if the opening is ¼ inch or so out of square. As a final check, set the window in the opening and check it for square.

13 Once you are certain the opening is correct, use a drill equipped with a long ½-inch spade bit to bore locator holes to the outside at each corner.

INSTALLING A WOOD WINDOW

These instructions are for a window with no nailing flange. (If your window has a flange, see pages 104–105.) Most unflanged windows are made of wood, and most have brick molding. For the three ways to install a window and its outside trim, see page 80.

When ordering a window be sure to specify a jamb of the correct width. If your walls have 2×4 studs and ½-inch exterior sheathing, the jambs should be 3⅝ inches wide (the extra ⅛ inch allows for imperfections). For a wall with 2×6 studs, a jamb width of 5⅝ inches is correct.

Unpack the window and inspect it before installing. Make sure all the weatherstripping is in good shape and the mechanisms and sashes operate smoothly.

Check with your building department to find which method of wrapping the opening is preferred; some departments have stringent requirements.

PRESTART CHECKLIST

☐ **TIME**
Once the opening is framed, about 3 hours to seal the opening and install a window and its exterior trim; also allow time for finishing the interior wall and installing interior trim (pages 100–103).

☐ **TOOLS**
Tape measure, hammer, nail set, level, stapler, caulk gun, drill with screwdriver bit, flat pry bar, handsaw, reciprocating saw, tin snips

☐ **SKILLS**
Careful fitting, driving nails or screws, checking for level and plumb

☐ **PREP**
Frame the opening and check for square (pages 88–95).

☐ **MATERIALS**
10d nails or 2-inch deck or wood screws, 8d casing nails, 6d finish nails, wood putty, shims, insulation, exterior caulk, roofing felt or building wrap, staples

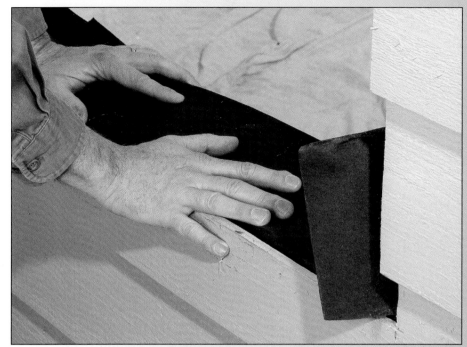

1 Cut strips of roofing felt or building wrap and cover the bottom of the rough opening. Later (steps 7–9) you will install additional wrapping and/or flashing.

FLASHING A WINDOW

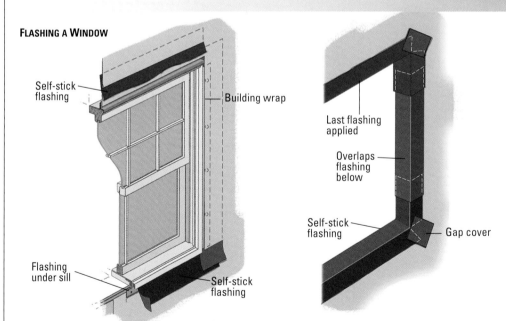

Self-stick flashing

Building wrap

Flashing under sill

Self-stick flashing

Last flashing applied

Overlaps flashing below

Self-stick flashing

Gap cover

Newer building techniques have specific requirements for flashing a window. In general the upper pieces should overlap the lower pieces so water can flow downward without seeping in. When installing a window in new construction (left), the building wrap overlaps the self-stick flashing.

In a remodel situation (right), a simpler arrangement is often used. Self-stick flashing is installed to the bottom, then the sides, then the top. Finally small pieces of flashing are applied over the V-shaped gaps at the corners.

2 Set the window temporarily in place, check for level, and shim the bottom as needed. If your window calls for installing a thick flashing with a piece of plywood at the bottom (see page 84), install it first or raise the window by the same thickness.

3 Tap in shims at the sides, checking for plumb as you go. Don't wedge the shims too tightly, or the jambs will warp. Use the level as a straightedge to confirm that the jamb has not warped.

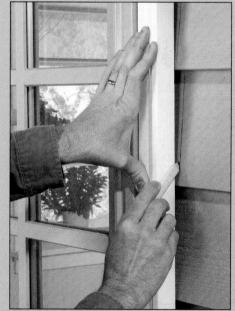

4 Make sure the window operates smoothly with the shims in place. Watch the alignment of the sash against the jambs as you move it. Adjust the shims as needed.

5 Tack (partially drive) nails or screws near the shims to hold the window temporarily in place.

6 On the outside, trace around the brick molding to mark the siding for cutting. Cut the siding (see page 83).

Drip cap flashing

7 Pry back the siding and install the felt, building wrap, or self-adhesive flashing. Cut pieces of felt or self-adhesive flashing to fit along the sides. Slip them in behind the siding, fold them over the studs, and staple. Cut a piece 6 inches longer than the width of the opening and install it the same way. Cut slits at the corners.

8 The slits cut on all four corners create V-shaped openings in the felt or flashing. Cover these with small pieces of felt or self-stick flashing.

9 If your window calls for it, use tin snips to cut a piece of metal drip cap flashing and slip it under the felt at the header.

WHAT IF...
You're installing a window in brick?

If you have a brick wall, hire a professional mason to cut the opening for you. The window attaches to the wood framing behind the brick veneer with metal masonry clips. You'll have to purchase the clips separately and attach them to your window jamb with deck screws.

Check window action

When the window is fully installed but before you trim it out, check that the window opens smoothly and easily. Especially with double-hung windows, it is easy to shim too tightly, causing the sashes to bind. To remove a shim, split it from the exposed end with a chisel. Leave the nail in place; set it after you have placed new shims.

10 Set the window back in place, with the brick molding tight against the felt or flashing. Inside, the front of the jambs should be flush with the finished wall. (Where you have not yet installed new drywall, the jambs should be ½ inch proud of the framing.)

11 Again shim the bottom and sides, check for level and square, and check that the window operates smoothly. Following manufacturer's directions (you may need to remove pieces of trim first), partially drive 6d finishing nails through the jambs to attach the window.

12 Outside, drive galvanized casing nails to attach the brick molding. Caulk between the trim and the window and between the trim and the siding.

13 Use a nail set to drive the finishing nails slightly below the surface of the wood. Where these nails are not covered with trim, apply wood putty to the resulting holes.

14 Use a handsaw to cut the shims flush with the studs, so you can install the drywall up against the jambs.

15 Gently stuff fiberglass insulation into the gaps around the jambs or fill the gaps with nonexpanding spray foam insulation. Expanding foam could warp the window frame.

TRIMMING OUT A WINDOW

Before you start trimming a window, finish the surrounding walls. If you cut out a large opening for installing a new window, that probably means you need to install new drywall. Attach the drywall and apply three coats of joint compound, sanding between each coat. (See *Stanley Interior Walls* or *Stanley Complete Drywall* for detailed drywall finishing instructions.)

If you will stain the new trim, paint the wall first. Apply stain and finish to the trim before installing it, so you will only have to touch up the cut ends and nail holes later. If you will paint the trim, you can paint the wall after the trim is installed.

The jambs must be flush with the wall surface. If the jambs do not extend out to the wall surface, install strips of wood to extend the jambs outward. If the jambs are proud of the wall, plane them down.

PRESTART CHECKLIST

☐ **TIME**
About 2 hours to install basic window trim; more time is required for more complicated situations.

☐ **TOOLS**
Tape measure, hammer or power nailer, nail set, hand miter box with backsaw or power miter box, jigsaw, level, combination square, drill

☐ **SKILLS**
Careful measuring and precise cutting

☐ **PREP**
Install the window and the surrounding wall surface.

☐ **MATERIALS**
The casing and stool material of your choice; 3d, 6d, and 8d finish nails; wood putty

Installing the stool

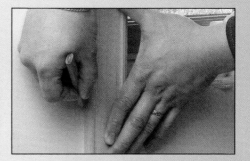
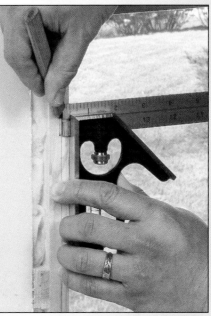

1 Use a combination square to draw the reveal on the edge of all the jambs. This is the width of the jamb edge—usually ¼ inch—that will not be covered by the casing. Set the square and hold the pencil tip against it as you slide the square along the jamb.

2 To determine the length of the stool, hold a piece of casing flat on the wall, one side aligned with the reveal line. Make a light mark on the wall (top). Turn the casing on edge and make a mark one casing thickness away from the first mark (bottom). Do this on the other side as well. The distance between the two outer lines is the length of the stool.

DESIGN OPTIONS

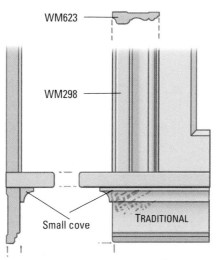

WM623

WM298

Small cove

TRADITIONAL

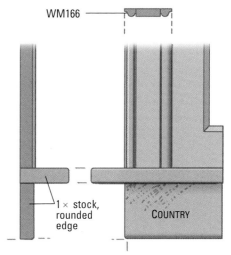

WM166

1 × stock, rounded edge

COUNTRY

Choose an ensemble of casing, stool, and other molding pieces. You can use single pieces of trim for the casing and apron or build a richer look by combining two or more pieces.

Here are designs that reflect traditional, country, and (opposite page) Victorian styles. Aprons can be made of any knot-free stock; round the edge with a sanding block. If you

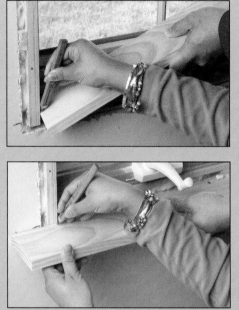

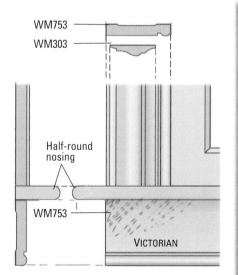

3 Cut the stool to length. To mark for the notch at each side, first mark for the depth of each notch (top) and then mark for their length (bottom).

4 Use a jigsaw (shown) or handsaw to cut the notches. Adjust the jigsaw blade so it slightly undercuts—that is, so it cuts slightly more from the bottom of the piece than from the top.

5 Set the stool in place and check for a tight fit all around; you may need to plane or saw it to make slight adjustments. Drill pilot holes and drive 8d finish nails to firmly attach the stool to the rough sill.

WM753

WM303

Half-round
nosing

WM753

VICTORIAN

plan to paint the trim, you can take advantage of the many style options available in medium density fiberboard (MDF) and plastic trim. The molding profile numbers shown are widely used.

WHAT IF...
You want a finished edge to an ornate apron?

A straight cut to both ends of an ornate apron looks amateurish. Here's a better approach. Hold the apron stock across the opening and mark where it intersects at the two outermost edges of the side casing. Miter-cut both ends. Next make miter cuts on a scrap of the same material. Cut the miter first, then make the straight cut so the resulting wedge is as long as the apron is thick. Glue the wedge piece in place to make a return—a finished end—for the molding. Fasten the apron by drilling pilot holes and using 6d finish nails every 12 inches.

Attaching casing

1 Cut one side of the head (top) casing piece to 45 degrees. Hold it in place, the cut edge aligned with the reveal line on one side, and mark for cutting on the other side. Tack (drive nails partway) the head casing piece into place.

2 To mark for a side casing, cut one end to 45 degrees. Hold it upside down, with the tip of the cut end resting on the outside edge of the sill, and mark the other end for a straight 90-degree cut at the top edge of the head casing.

3 Hold the casing pieces together. Install the casing with 6d finishing nails into studs and 3d finishing nails into the jamb. When you drive a nail near an edge, drill a pilot hole first to prevent splitting the wood.

4 To help ensure a tight and durable fit at the miter, drive a 3d nail horizontally to lock one piece against the other.

Block casing

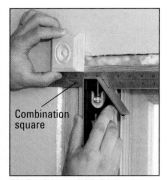

Combination square

Casing

Nail set

Block casing, which features a square rosette at the upper corners, adds a decorative touch and is easy to install because there are no miter joints.

Draw the reveal lines. Squirt a dab of construction adhesive onto the back of each rosette,

carefully place it at the corner of the lines, and hold a square against it as you partially drive a nail to hold it in place.

Cut casing pieces to fit between the rosettes and the sill. Install with 6d and 3d finishing nails.

WHAT IF…
You have problem joints?

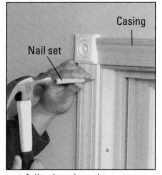

If a miter joint is not tight, use a plane or knife to shave the miter; undercut so the bottom of the cut is deeper than the top. It sometimes helps to slip a small shim under one or both of the pieces. Or start installing the

side piece with the miter tight but the piece going at an angle; straighten the piece as you drive nails farther down.

If a jamb is proud of the wall, use a plane to shave it down.

Picture frame casing

1 If the window has no stool, draw reveal lines on all four jambs. (You may need to install jamb extensions on the bottom jamb.) Cut one side of each of the side casing pieces and mark for cutting the other side.

2 Tack the side casing pieces in place. Fasten the pieces at each end, being careful to line them up with the reveal lines.

3 Set the top piece upside down on the tips of the side casing pieces and mark for the miter cuts. Do the same for the bottom.

4 On a large work surface, glue, clamp, and nail the pieces together. If one miter joint is not tight, you can slightly adjust the others to make it tighter. Apply the frame as one piece.

INSTALLING A FLANGED WINDOW

Metal and vinyl windows have an integral flange (also known as a nailing fin) that attaches to the house. Once the flange is firmly fastened, there is no need to anchor the window jamb.

Carefully seal the house's sheathing correctly so water flows away from the house and cannot be trapped next to the sheathing. The sealing instructions on these pages will suit most situations, but your window may come with different instructions or your local building department may have different requirements. See pages 82–85 for a more elaborate sealing system.

Choose a metal or vinyl window that feels solid when you try to twist it and has substantial weatherstripping. Buy from a well-established manufacturer so you can easily buy replacement weatherstripping and other parts if needed in the future.

For instructions on cutting and framing the opening, see pages 88–95. Check that the opening is square (see page 76).

PRESTART CHECKLIST

☐ **TIME**
Several hours (working with a helper if the window is large) to install the window and trim

☐ **TOOLS**
Tape measure, drill, hammer, level, stapler, caulk gun

☐ **SKILLS**
Basic carpentry skills

☐ **PREP**
Cut the opening and check for square. Buy a flanged window to fit.

☐ **MATERIALS**
Window, exterior casing, shims, caulk, roofing felt or building paper, drip cap flashing, other flashing (such as self-stick) if required by codes, finishing nails, staples, galvanized roofing nails

1 Set the window in the opening, pressed against the siding, and drive a screw at the center of the top flange. Shim as needed so the window is square and the sashes work smoothly and are aligned with the frame. Drive three or four more screws through the flanges to hold the window in place temporarily.

2 To mark for cutting back the siding, hold pieces of exterior trim against the window and scribe along the siding with a pencil. Cut the siding as shown on page 83. Keep the blade on the outside of the cutline, so the opening will be about 1/8 inch wider than the casing.

PROTECTING THE HOUSE FROM MOISTURE

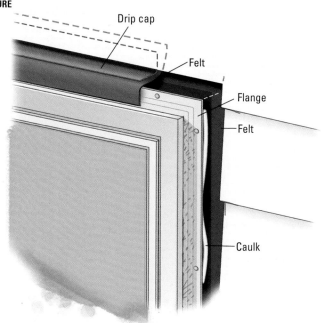

In this arrangement felt or building paper is first stapled to the sheathing, with the top pieces overlapping the lower pieces. A bead of caulk is applied to the felt and the window is set in the caulk. Next comes another layer of building paper, installed like the first layer. At the top, metal drip cap flashing is tucked up under the siding and on top of the second layer of felt, and the exterior casing is installed just under the drip cap.

Drip cap

Felt

Flange

Felt

Caulk

3 Cut 10- to 12-inch-wide strips of roofing felt or building paper. Slip them behind the siding, wrap them around the framing, and staple in place. First install the piece at the sill, then the sides, then the top piece. Finally cut four pieces about 4 inches square and slip them into the corners to cover the V-shape gaps.

4 Apply a bead of caulk all around the opening, where the flange will be. Tilt the window into place. Drive a screw near the center of the top flange and shim. Check for level and operation as in step 1. Make sure the casing will fit all around the window.

5 Once the window is correctly aligned, drive roofing nails into the nail holes and remove the screw. (Nails are preferred because screw heads are bulky, making it difficult to install the casing.)

6 Cut a strip of roofing felt or building paper 8 inches wide, slip it under the siding above the window, and staple it in place.

7 Cut pieces of exterior casing to fit and nail them in place with 10d casing (exterior finishing) nails. Caulk around the casing and on the joint between the casing and the window. Prime and paint.

8 Cut drip cap (for metal drip-cap flashing, see page 98) to cover the casing. Apply a bead of caulk just below the siding and slip the drip cap up under the siding. Nail 4d galvanized nails down into the casing.

INSTALLING A BAY WINDOW

The farther a bay window protrudes from the house, the more dramatic the effect and the more it opens a room. You can choose among units that protrude at 45-, 30-, or 10-degree angles; the latter is sometimes called a bow window. Individual windows may be fixed, double-hung, or casement.

A bay unit attaches like a standard flanged window but with some important differences. Some units also require support from above using cables that attach to framing members in the eaves or the wall above. Some require support from below using brackets or a knee wall. Some need both types of support. A smaller bow window may not need this type of support and can be installed much like a standard flanged window (pages 104–105).

Plan how you will finish the top and bottom of the bay window. You may be able to purchase a ready-made roof or you may need to custom-build one (see page 108). The bottom is usually easy to trim out, but you may choose to build a wall down to the ground. In these the roof and skirt are built on the ground and then installed.

PRESTART CHECKLIST

☐ **TIME**
A day or two depending on trimwork

☐ **TOOLS**
Tape measure, drill, hammer, level, stapler, caulk gun, screwdriver, flat pry bar, circular saw

☐ **SKILLS**
Good carpentry skills

☐ **PREP**
Cut the opening and check for square. You will need one or two strong helpers.

☐ **MATERIALS**
Bay window, exterior casing, 2×4s, shims, caulk, roofing felt or building paper, drip cap, flashing, plywood, roofing, finishing nails, staples, roofing nails, interior trim, casing nails, insulation

Attaching the window

1 Cut and frame an opening as shown on pages 90–95. Flash the opening (see page 96). The jambs of the window shown fasten directly to framing members. Some other bay windows have flanges; with such units you'll need to set the window in temporarily, shim it square, mark for cutting the siding to accommodate the casing, and cut the siding (see pages 104–105).

CABLE SUPPORT ARRANGEMENTS

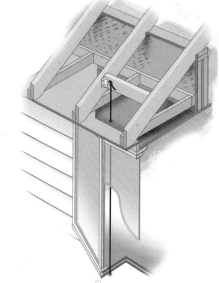
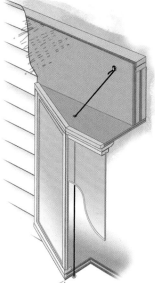

Read the instructions carefully and be sure to install the required cable support. In one arrangement the cables are attached to an overhanging eaves structure. Cable attached to a header or studs must be at an angle no flatter than 30 degrees. Whichever method you choose, plan how you will cover the cables with a roof or a short wall up to the eaves. Some units have cables preinstalled; with others you have to add the hardware for the cable yourself.

2 Following the manufacturer's instructions mark the fastener locations. Drill four or so holes in the unit to allow you to firmly fasten it in place for shimming and leveling. (You'll later bore holes for plugs to cover the final fasteners—see step 2 on page 110.)

3 Cut a pair of temporary supports (see page 83). With a helper or two, raise the window into place and temporarily support it. Check for level and plumb all around and shim as needed. Drive screws at the top and sides to temporarily hold the window in place. Check that operable windows open smoothly.

4 Make a template or carefully measure so you can prefab the roof. It is much easier to finetune the angled cuts and install the pieces while working at ground level. Drill large holes for the support cables. Measure and cut the final sheathing pieces (to be installed in step 4 on page 109).

5 Set the roof in place and mark where you'll cut the siding to allow for the flashing. Use a spacer to mark for adequate flashing space. If needed mark the siding for cutting, remove the window, and cut the siding.

Insulating and finishing the exterior

1 Attach the cable brackets. Make sure the brackets are roughly in line with the cable attachment points on the window. Screws should be driven deep into framing members, not just the siding.

2 While checking for level adjust the mounting hardware as needed. Raise the outside of the unit slightly so it is higher than level to allow for settling.

3 Fill the framing with insulation. Cut a piece of fiberglass insulation to fit on top of the window, then cut a slightly smaller piece to rest on top of the first piece. Fill the rest of the cavity with loose fiberglass.

FRAMING A ROOF

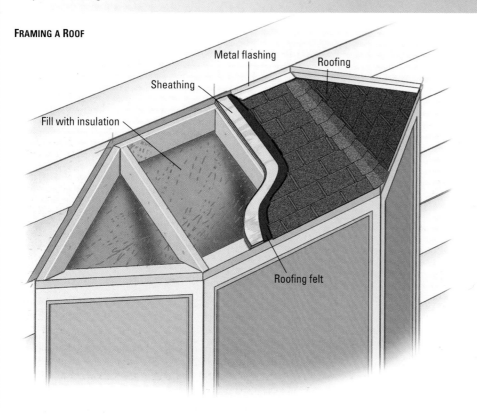

- Metal flashing
- Roofing
- Sheathing
- Fill with insulation
- Roofing felt

WHAT IF...
Your bay window is beneath an overhang?
If the window is under an overhang, you can install framing on top of the window, attaching framing to the wall and on the underside of the overhang. If there is no overhang, build a roof as shown or purchase a prefabricated roof, if available in the size you need.

Though small, the roof over a bay window has all the components of a standard roof. Framing is made of 2×4s or 2×2s. Start by attaching the pieces against the wall, then cut the rafters to the required angles and install them. Attach ¹/₂-inch plywood sheathing, add a metal drip edge at the bottom, and cover with roofing felt. Install the shingles and then slip a piece of metal drip cap under the siding and over the shingles.

4 Add the sheathing pieces cut earlier, fastening them with 8d cement-coated sinker nails or 2-inch screws. Finish it by adding flashing and drip edge, then roofing felt and shingles.

5 Prefab the skirt as well. The complexity of the joints makes it much easier to build the skirt on a work surface rather than on the window itself. The framing shown is made of 2×4s, which will allow for 3½ inches of insulation under the window. Attach the plywood bottom. Attach trim to cover the framing.

6 Tack insulation under the window. Cut a piece of plywood to cover the bottom. Bore holes in the plywood so you can tighten the cable nuts later if needed. Attach the framing to the underside of the window using screws. If there will be a short wall down to the ground, pour a small concrete pad and add matching framing on the pad.

WHAT IF...
You need knee braces?

If required, or if you like the look, add knee braces at the bottom. A decorative wood brace like this attaches using lag screws driven into wall studs. These were made from two pieces of 2×12, laminated with glue and cut to shape with a band saw. Readymade braces are available at most home centers.

Trimming the bay window

1 Add facia to the skirt. Make the angled cuts with a table saw, power mitersaw, or a circular saw. These angles can be difficult; always try the joint before cutting the piece to final length so you can recut the angle if needed. Tack each piece in place using 6d galvanized box nails. Complete the final nailing only when you are satisfied with all the joints.

2 Complete the fastening of the jambs and seat. For a clean finish, bore countersinks to hide the screw heads. Use a Forstner bit to make a clean hole. Purchase wood plugs for the holes.

WHAT IF…
Your window comes with a seat and jamb extenders?

Some windows come with a seat board and jamb extenders. The seat board is similar to a standard window stool. If it juts out too far, cut it with a table saw or circular saw and sand the edges. You may need to shim the underside of the seat board using strips of 1/4-inch plywood. Attach the seat board with construction adhesive and a few finishing nails placed where they will be covered by trim boards. Install the headboard as well.

The jamb extension pieces sent with your window may have to be rip-cut to fit. Hold an extension in place and scribe it along the wall surface. Rip-cut the jamb extensions to the correct width. Insert insulating foam rods into the spaces where the jamb extensions will go.

6 Tack pieces of casing in place and measure for the length of the apron. Fasten the apron to the seat board with finishing nails. (If your unit has a seat with a finished edge that extends beyond the wall, place the apron under the seat.) For how to finish the ends of the apron, see page 101.

3 Make a final check for level and plumb all around. Adjust the shims accordingly. Check again that the windows operate smoothly and are aligned with the frames. Fasten the screws in place.

4 Apply carpenter's glue to the plugs and set them in the fastener holes. Gently tap the caps until they are flush with the surface; most are tapered for this purpose. Once the glue dries, lightly sand the caps.

5 Stuff insulation into the gaps between the side and top jambs and the house framing. Stuff gently but fill the spaces completely. Or use nonexpanding foam insulation (see page 175).

7 Install the casing, following instructions on pages 102–103. Fill all the nail holes with wood putty, sand smooth, and apply finish or paint.

8 Install the opener cranks or other hardware and the window screens.

STANLEY PRO TIP

Trim simplified
Measure the thickness of your wall— the drywall or plaster, plus the sheathing and perhaps the siding or stucco—and order jamb extensions and other pieces that will require as little modification as possible.

When you install the window, ensure that the jamb extensions and the headboard will be flush with the interior wall surface. You may be able to move the window out or in to minimize custom cutting of trim. Many bay windows come with nailing flanges, but these flanges actually do little to hold the window in place, so you can cut the flange off if you need to move the window in or out.

INSTALLING A ROUND WINDOW

Framing for a round, octagonal, oval, or half-round window starts the same as for a standard window. Cut and frame a rectangular opening (pages 88–95) to accommodate the window at its greatest dimensions—in this case the top of a half-round window's arc.

The installation of the round window shown here includes sheathing with self-adhesive flashing tape. There is no metal drip cap (see page 98, step 9) over the rounded top; the joint between the curved brick molding and the siding is simply caulked. For a more weatherproof installation, have a roofer or a sheet metal shop make up a curved drip cap to fit your window.

With a flanged window like the one shown, it often makes sense to remove a section of siding so pieces that overlap the flange can be woven in (see page 30).

For curved cuts through heavy materials, a reciprocating saw is nearly indispensable. You can rent one if you don't own one.

PRESTART CHECKLIST

☐ **TIME**
With a rectangular opening cut, about 3 hours to frame and install a half-round window

☐ **TOOLS**
Tape measure, hammer, drill, scribing compass, reciprocating saw, circular saw or power miter box, stapler

☐ **SKILLS**
Measuring; framing; using a circular saw, jigsaw, and reciprocating saw

☐ **PREP**
Cut and frame the opening on the inside, but do not cut the sheathing.

☐ **MATERIALS**
Round-topped window, cardboard for a template, 2×4s for angled framing pieces, roofing felt or building paper, self-stick flashing tape, nails and screws

1 Place the window onto a piece of cardboard and trace its outline. Cut the cardboard along the line with a utility knife.

2 Tape the template to the sheathing and mark for cutting the opening.

FLASHING A ROUND-TOPPED WINDOW

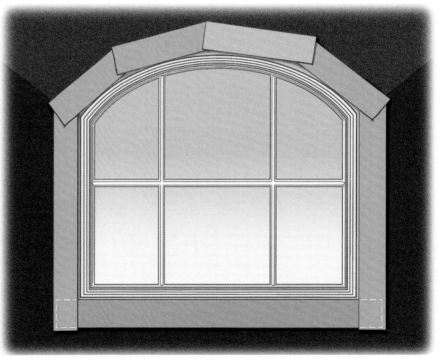

After wrapping the window framing with roofing felt or building paper (see pages 96 and 104), apply pieces of roofing felt or self-stick flashing tape to the front as shown. Flashing tape is preferred but is sometimes difficult to install under existing siding.

3 Bore an access hole and use a reciprocating saw to cut the opening. Cut to the outside of the line so the opening will be 1/4 inch larger than the window.

4 To measure for a short framing piece with 45-degree cuts on either end, hold a layout square against the stud and measure along its edge toward the header.

5 Use a power mitersaw or a circular saw to cut the piece with a 45-degree bevel at each end. Test the fit; it should be just outside the curved cutout. Drive nails to install it.

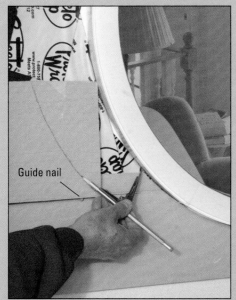

Guide nail

6 Remove the siding so you can weave it in (see page 30). Add flashing, working from the bottom up. Install the window as shown on page 105. To mark the new siding, scribe with a compass. To keep the desired overlap, set each piece on partially driven guide nails. Hold the compass level as you mark.

7 Cut the siding using a jigsaw. Try the fit after cutting, rescribing with the compass as needed. Once you are satisfied with the fit, hold the siding in place and mark its length for cutting.

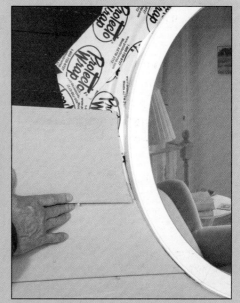

8 Apply a bead of caulk where the piece will be applied and nail it in place using 6d galvanized nails. When all the siding is installed, caulk around the window.

INSTALLING A TUBE SKYLIGHT

A standard skylight (pages 116–119) is difficult to install when the ceiling does not follow the roof line. A tube skylight enables you to bring natural sunlight into a flat-ceiling room with relative ease. You won't have to cut through framing or install new framing.

The metal tube for the type shown here assembles like ductwork. A variety of elbow fittings are available to make turns. Some units have flexible tubing for installation in hard-to-reach areas.

Some models offer an electric light that fits into the tube to provide overhead lighting at night and some can control the amount of sunlight that comes in. Those upgrades call for adding an electrical circuit and making electrical connections.

The most crucial part of the job takes place on the roof. Follow manufacturer's instructions carefully to ensure that the unit will not leak.

PRESTART CHECKLIST

☐ **TIME**
About half a day to install a tubed skylight with one or two turns in the ducting

☐ **TOOLS**
Tape measure, hammer, drill, flat pry bar, putty knife, drywall saw, screwdriver, reciprocating saw, utility knife

☐ **SKILLS**
Measuring, sawing, working at heights

☐ **PREP**
Determine where you want the skylight and check that the attic space above is unobstructed.

☐ **MATERIALS**
Tubed skylight, ductwork (tubing), elbows as needed, sheet metal screws, duct tape or tape provided by manufacturer, roofing cement

1 Drill a hole where you want the skylight to be and poke a wire up into the attic. Find the wire in the attic and drill a hole nearby, centered between two joists so there will be room for the tubing.

2 Trace the outline of the ceiling ring on the ceiling, with the locator hole in the center. Cut the opening using a drywall saw or saber saw. Attach the ceiling ring using the hardware provided that grips the drywall from behind.

THREE POSSIBLE ANGLES

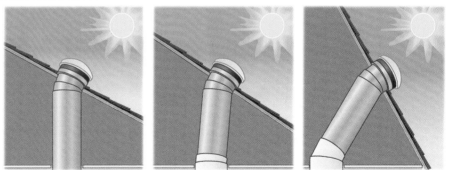

The shorter and straighter the tubing run, the brighter the sunlight in the room. However, because the interior of the tube is mirrorlike, it will transmit adequate light even if the run is long and makes several bends. Most kits have a couple of adjustable elbows; additional elbows and straight runs can be purchased as needed. Once you reach the roof sheathing, you will probably need an elbow to help the roof unit lie flat.

3 Start assembling the tube in the attic. Start with an elbow at the bottom and add pieces of tubing until you are near the roof. Center the tube between two rafters. Drive a nail up through the roof to indicate the center of the roof unit.

4 Caution: Prepare a safe and secure working platform on the roof. Using the unit's flange as a template, mark for cutting a round hole in the roof. Use a crayon or chalk to mark on darker roofing.

5 Drill an access hole with a ¾-inch spade bit. Use a reciprocating saw to cut the hole, guiding it around the outside of the cutline to give yourself some wiggle room during installation.

6 Check manufacturer's instructions for how much roofing to remove. Use a flat pry bar to pry out roofing nails and remove shingles as needed.

7 Slip the flange under shingles and felt at the top, and align its hole with the hole in the roof. Reinstall shingles around the flange and cut them to produce a ⅝-inch gap around the ring.

8 Inside the attic, seal all the joints by driving sheet metal screws and wrapping the joints with duct tape.

9 On the ceiling below attach the diffuser lens.

INSTALLING A SKYLIGHT

A standard skylight provides plenty of ambient light and even a view of the sky, making a room seem more spacious and airy. However, installation is more difficult. This section shows installing a skylight where the ceiling follows the roofline. If you have a flat ceiling, you will need to build a light shaft, which involves framing and covering with drywall (see the box on page 119).

A fixed-pane skylight is the least expensive option, but an openable or venting skylight will help cool a room in the summer. Or choose a unit with a built-in shade or blinds. You can even buy a skylight with a motor that opens and closes the unit or its shade or blinds; the motor can be controlled with a wall switch and/or it may operate automatically. Installing a motorized unit calls for fairly extensive electrical work.

In this section, a typical skylight is installed. Your window may have different installation requirements, so pay close attention to the manufacturer's instructions.

PRESTART CHECKLIST

☐ **TIME**
A full day to install and trim a skylight; more time if you need to build a shaft

☐ **TOOLS**
Tape measure, stud sensor, drill, hammer, level, stapler, caulk gun, framing square, screwdriver, flat pry bar, reciprocating saw, utility knife, tin snips, drywall saw

☐ **SKILLS**
Good carpentry skills

☐ **PREP**
Arrange to work on the roof safely and protect the floor in the room below with a drop cloth. Enlist a helper.

☐ **MATERIALS**
Skylight, 2× lumber, molding, drywall, nails or screws, roofing cement, caulk, insulating foam

1 Use a stud sensor to find the rafters. Plan how you will frame the opening (see options on opposite page). Use a drywall saw (or a reciprocating saw, if the ceiling is plaster and lath) to cut a hole wide enough to accommodate the framing (including the headers, which may be single or double 2×s).

2 Unless the unit is narrow enough to fit between rafters, you will need to cut at least one rafter. Before you cut into a rafter, support it temporarily on either side. For each support, screw a piece of 2×6 to the ceiling and cut a piece of 2×4 to fit snugly between the floor and the 2×6.

FLASHING A SKYLIGHT

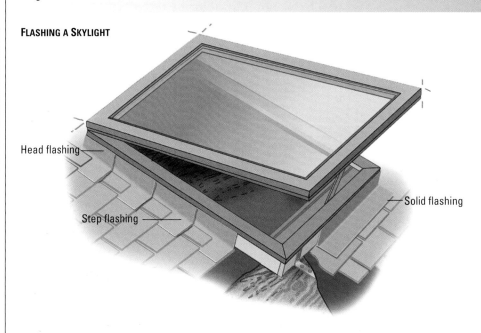

Head flashing

Solid flashing

Step flashing

The skylight installation shown here uses a combination of step and solid flashing. Other types may have solid flashing on all sides or may call for cutting back or removing shingles around the opening (not required by the window shown). Some may need a header with only a single 2× rather than double 2× s as shown in these steps.

3 Mark the rafter to be cut for the rough opening dimension. Draw lines either 1½ or 3 inches to account for the thickness of a single or double header at each end. Use a square to draw a right-angle line along each rafter and cut carefully using a reciprocating saw, then a handsaw. Do not cut into the roof sheathing.

4 Install framing as needed (see right). Use 2× lumber that is the same thickness as your rafters. For double headers cut the pieces and nail or screw them together on the floor, then install. Check that the opening is the correct size and ensure it is square.

5 Drill a ¾-inch hole up through the roof at each corner. Use a reciprocating saw to cut through the roof alongside the framing. Cut slowly; you may have to cut through several nails.

6 Caution: Arrange a safe place to work on the roof. Roof jacks are often the best solution. Gently pry up—but do not remove—roofing all around the opening. Remove nails so you can slip in roofing felt all around and flashings at the bottom and top.

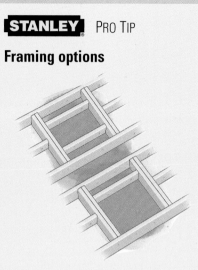

The framing configuration depends on the size of the skylight and the spacing of the rafters (typically either 24 or 16 inches on center, meaning they have either 22½- or 14½-inch spaces between them). If you do not need to locate the skylight in a precise spot, you can probably use at least one of the existing rafters as part of the framing.

Follow installation instructions carefully. Some gaps between the skylight and the roofing can be sealed using roofing cement, but it is important that the flashings, roofing felt, and shingles be installed correctly, so water runs down the roof and cannot seep in between the layers of roofing materials.

Some units require cutting back the shingles around the opening, installing the flashings, and reinstalling the roofing.

With some units the bottom flashing piece is installed before the step flashing (steps 11 and 12).

7 Trimming below the skylight will call for some custom woodworking. The easiest approach is to carefully measure (and then measure again) the depth of jamb you'll need. Prefab a finished jamb and confirm the fit on the bottom of the skylight. Confirm that it will fit inside the framing. (See Step 14 for final installation.)

8 Cut strips of roofing felt (tar paper) the width of the rafters plus 8 inches. Starting at the bottom and working up, slip the felt under the shingles and the existing felt, wrap around the rafters, and staple against the rafters. You will need to cut slits at the corners.

9 Slip the head flashing piece under the shingles at the top. You may need to pull or cut some roofing nails to do this.

STANLEY PRO TIP

Trim options

If you have 2×6 or 2×8 rafters, trim can be made from 1×8 or 1×10 lumber, but for larger rafters plywood may be your best option. You can buy oak plywood if the trim will be oak. If you plan to paint, use birch plywood, which is easier to paint than standard pine or fir.

For stained trim, cover the partially exposed edge of the plywood with iron-on strips of wood veneer. Consider staining the jamb box before installing it; any work you can do at ground level instead of over your head is to your advantage.

Framing for a skylight with a shaft

If the ceiling is flat, you will need to build a frame for a shaft. The shaft may point straight down, be angled, or be splayed (larger at the ceiling than at the roof).

The shaft framing is not structural; it need only be strong enough to support the drywall that will be attached to it. Cut pieces of 2×4 to fit between the bottom of the roof opening and the top of the ceiling opening; you will need to make some odd angled cuts. Attach with angle-driven screws or nails. Apply fiberglass insulation around the outside and cover the inside of the shaft with drywall.

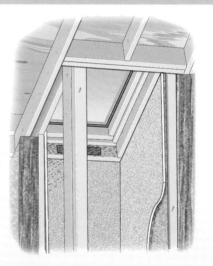

10 Have someone help you lift the skylight through the opening and position it. Partially drive a couple of screws or nails below the opening to temporarily support the skylight. Check from inside the room to see that the unit is centered, then drive screws through the brackets to secure the skylight.

11 Install step flashing, working from the bottom up. Slip each piece under a shingle, aligned with the bottom edge of the shingle, then drive roofing nails to attach the flashing and the shingle. Flashing and shingles should always overlap the next piece lower on the roof.

12 Install the bottom flashing piece (also called counterflashing) following manufacturer's instructions. Part of the bottom piece may slip over the step flashing and part may slip under. Drive screws to attach the bottom flashing.

13 Seal the joint between the roofing and the skylight with caulk or plastic roofing cement.

14 Shim your prefab jamb box in place using 8d finishing nails. Fill any gaps between the framing and the jamb using caulk or foam spray insulation.

15 By using beefy casing you may be able to avoid drywall patching; otherwise, patch and tape drywall as needed. Then cut and install picture-frame style casing (see page 103).

Door Repairs And Upgrades

Doors are less complicated than windows, but they are opened and closed more often. As a result most homes have one or more doors that do not close easily and tightly and are in need of some repair.

In most cases the problem can be diagnosed with a quick inspection. The door may be rubbing against the frame on the side or the top, or against the threshold at the bottom. The latch may be malfunctioning or the bolt may not be aligned with the strike. Often one or more screws in a hinge may be loose.

Most door repairs can be performed in less than an hour. If the door itself needs to be cut or planed, a larger investment of time is required. If a door is coming apart or warping, it usually needs to be replaced, as shown in the next chapter.

This chapter starts with repairs to interior room doors, which are the ones most likely to have problems. Most of the techniques shown for interior doors also apply to exterior doors. You'll also find out how to repair storm doors, sliders, and closet doors, as well as how to replace a threshold and a sill.

Easy upgrades

You can easily improve a door's security or appearance by installing a new lock or handle. Installing new trim for interior or exterior doors is an easy way to change the look of a room or the front of the house. And if you have a door that lets in cold drafts, it can be made tighter and more energy-efficient by adding easy-to-install weatherstripping.

Most door problems can be fixed easily, quickly, and without special tools.

Chapter Preview

Troubleshooting door problems
page 122

Replacing a sill and threshold
page 130

Storm door repairs
page 132

Sliding patio door repairs
page 133

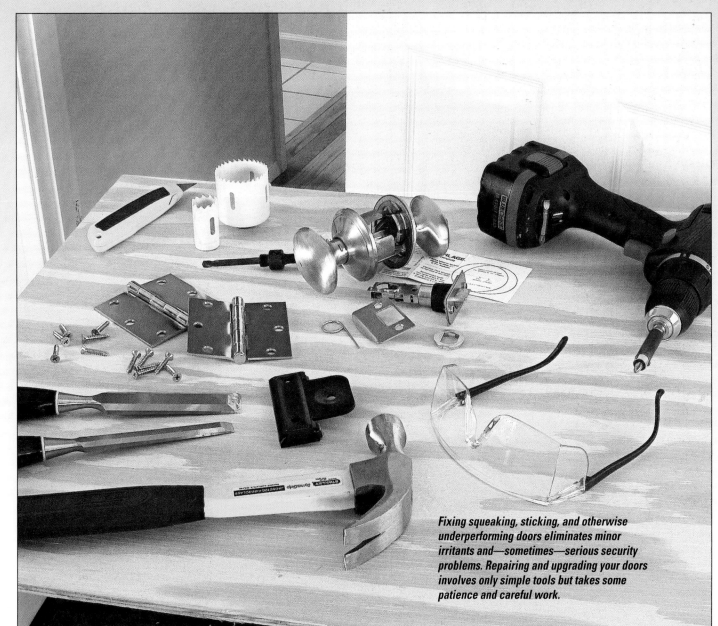

Fixing squeaking, sticking, and otherwise underperforming doors eliminates minor irritants and—sometimes—serious security problems. Repairing and upgrading your doors involves only simple tools but takes some patience and careful work.

Repairing bifold and sliding doors
page 134

Repairing old latches
page 136

Choosing replacement locks
page 137

Installing a lockset
page 138

Sprucing up an entry door with trim
Page 142

Weatherstripping a door
page 144

TROUBLESHOOTING DOOR PROBLEMS

To get that satisfying "thunk" when a door closes—rather than rattles, squeaks, or scrapes—there must be an even gap between the door and the jamb all around; the hinges should be flush with the jamb and move freely; and the **stop** and the **strike plate** should be correctly aligned, so the door's **latch** easily clicks into the hole in the strike plate when the door closes.

The door itself may be solid-core, hollow-core, or made of panels; see pages 20–23. **Hinges** are attached to the **jamb**, which is attached to the house's framing on the sides and above. An interior door usually has two hinges and a heavier exterior door usually has three. Usually there is a gap between the jamb and the framing, which is filled with shims positioned near the nails.

Stop molding is positioned so the door bumps against it when closed. If the stop is too tight, the door will be difficult to close; if it is too loose, the door will rattle. On the latch side of the jamb, a **strike plate** is positioned over a hole in the jamb; the door's **latch bolt** engages a hole in the strike plate to latch the door. On an exterior door there is often a dead-bolt lock as well. The holes and strike plate must be correctly positioned for the door to close properly.

Hinges are attached to the other edge of the door with screws. They grab effectively only in solid wood (not particleboard). Long screws can be used if the door is solid wood, but shorter screws are used for a hollow-core door or a solid-core door with a particleboard core.

A squeaky hinge may only need a squirt of the right lubricant. If you see rust, first use penetrating lubricant to free rusted parts. Then apply powdered graphite or silicone lubricant for a longer-lasting solution. Also use lubricants to free a balky latch bolt.

ANATOMY OF A DOOR

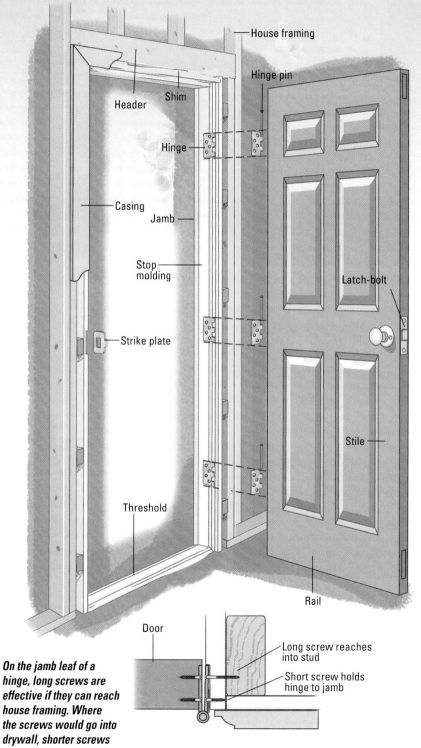

On the jamb leaf of a hinge, long screws are effective if they can reach house framing. Where the screws would go into drywall, shorter screws are just as good.

What door binding means

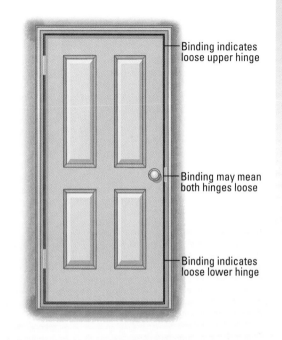

Binding indicates loose upper hinge

Binding may mean both hinges loose

Binding indicates loose lower hinge

A binding door may need to be planed (page 127), but often simpler repairs will solve the problem. If a door binds on the latch side at the top, the upper hinge may be loose; tighten the screws or repair the screw holes (page 124). If it binds on the latch side at the bottom, you may need to fix the bottom hinge screws.

If the door binds along the latch side, the hinges may need to be set deeper or the strike plate may need to be set deeper. If the hinge side binds, one or both hinges may need to be shimmed out (page 124).

If there is binding along the top or the bottom, the door needs to be planed or trimmed (page 127).

Troubleshooting a door

Problem	Solution
Binding on the latch side	Tighten any loose hinge screws (page 124). Plane if needed (page 127).
Binding on the top or bottom	Plane the door (page 127).
Binding on the hinge side	Scrape away paint buildup. Shim out hinges if they are not flush with the jamb (page 124). If needed, remove, plane, and recut the mortises for the hinges (pages 148–149).
Hinge squeaks	Apply penetrating oil, then graphite or silicone lubricant (page 126). If needed, disassemble the hinge and clean, or replace.
Loose doorknob	Tighten screws holding the handle and/or the escutcheon (faceplate).
Door latch won't close	If the latch is balky, clean away any paint and lubricate. If the latch bolt is not aligned with the strike plate, adjust the plate (page 126). If the door won't close far enough to reach the strike, adjust the stop (page 125).
Door has trouble closing all the way; hinge knuckles move when you close the door	Shim a hinge leaf (page 124) or bend the hinge with an adjustable wrench (page 124).
Door rattles when closed	Adjust the strike plate (page 126) and/or the stop (page 125).
Door sticks in humid weather	Plane the door, then seal the edges with paint or polyurethane.
Door scrapes at bottom, perhaps because of new flooring or carpeting	Cut the door (pages 128–129).

STANLEY PRO TIP

The latch-side bevel

On the latch side, a door is cut at a slight bevel to make it easier to close.

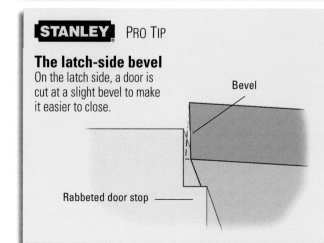

Bevel

Rabbeted door stop

Tightening a loose hinge

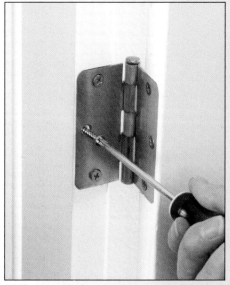

1 If a door binds, open it, grasp the knob, and lift up to see if a hinge is loose. If one is loose remove two or more screws and try driving in longer screws.

2 If that does not solve the problem, trim pieces of shim or other small wood pieces to fit tightly in the holes (matchsticks or golf tees work well). Tap the wood in and use a knife to cut it flush with the jamb.

3 Drill a pilot hole in the center, taking care to hold the drill level and straight as you work. Drive new screws. Check the door for binding and correct any problems; if the door sticks, the screws will come loose again.

Shimming a hinge

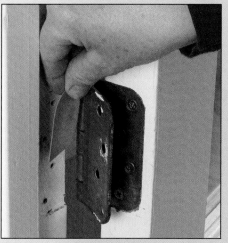

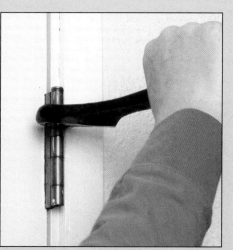

If a hinge leaf is recessed below the surface of the jamb or the door edge, the door will not close well and the hinge will bend when you close it. Use a hinge leaf as a template to make a cardboard shim that you can slip behind the leaf.

If the hinge leaf is recessed only at the bottom or the top, insert a shim behind only part of the hinge leaf.

You can adjust a door slightly to the left or the right by bending the hinge knuckles. With the door closed slip an adjustable wrench over the door leaf only—not the jamb leaf—and bend.

Adjusting a stop

1 If the stop is keeping the door from closing all the way or if it is too far away so that the door rattles, move the stop. First score the paint line where the stop meets the jamb. Then tap in two putty knives and begin prying.

2 When the separation is large enough, insert a flat pry bar. Keep one putty knife in place to avoid damaging the jamb. Gently work your way down the stop until you can remove it completely. Remove the nails.

3 With the door closed reposition the stop, place a cardboard shim between the stop and the door, and drive new nails. Touch up the paint as necessary.

Removing a door

1 To remove a door, support it at the bottom on the latch side with shims. Tap the pin up with a hammer and screwdriver and pull it out. On some hinges you must tap a nail up through the bottom of the hinge first.

2 With the pins removed you can simply pull the door out. Put the pins back into hinge leaves so you will not lose them.

WHAT IF...
The pin is stuck?

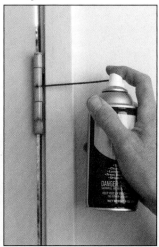

If a hinge pin is stuck and will not come out when you tap it with a screwdriver, first try squirting with penetrating lubricant. Wait about 10 minutes and try tapping again.

If it still will not come out, it may be easier to remove the screws from one leaf, which will allow you to remove the door.

A door that rattles

If a strike plate is recessed (as often happens when the doorway is painted several times), remove the screws, pull it out, and make cardboard shims to fit in the mortise. Use as many shims as needed to bring the strike flush with the jamb.

If the latch bolt does not align with the hole in the strike, preventing it from latching, you may be able to solve the problem by filing the strike plate.

If that does not solve the problem, move the strike plate. Use a knife and chisel to cut a mortise and enlarge the hole if needed. Drill pilot holes and reattach the strike plate. Fill the exposed mortise area with wood putty and sand smooth.

STANLEY PRO TIP: **Squeaky hinge**

It is usually easiest to replace a rusty hinge. However, if the hinge is of a style that is hard to replace, disassemble it and clean with solvent and a toothbrush. Allow to dry, then polish with very fine sandpaper. Apply lubricant (options above) and reassemble.

WHAT IF...
A door opens or closes itself?

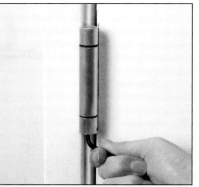

An older home may have a doorway that is out of square or out of plumb so that the door opens or closes by itself. Purchase a spring hinge, which can be adjusted to correct the problem.

Planing a binding door

1 If a door binds and a loose hinge is not the problem, close it until it just touches the jamb (don't force it closed) and use a pencil to scribe a line where the door needs to be trimmed. The ideal is a $\frac{1}{8}$-inch gap between the door and jamb at all points. Mark both sides of the door.

2 Adjust a plane so the blade barely protrudes beyond the base. Test on a scrap piece of wood; the plane should easily produce very thin shavings. Readjust as needed. You can use a shaping tool (page 25), but the resulting edge will require sanding to make it smooth.

3 Set the door on the floor so it is stable. Hold the plane flat on the door edge and press down as you push forward. Don't force the plane; use moderate pressure. Plane with the grain. If the plane chatters or gets stuck, plane in the opposite direction.

4 Plane down to the scribe lines. Sand the edge smooth and slightly round the corners with a sanding block. Finish the edge to match the door.

Planing the top or bottom of a door

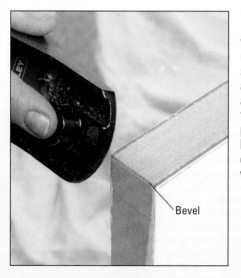

Bevel

1 At the top or bottom of a panel where the horizontal rails and vertical stiles meet, plane across, rather than along, the grain of the stile. First use the plane or a sanding block to bevel the outside edge so it won't splinter.

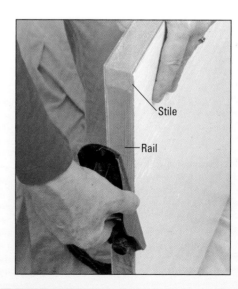

Stile

Rail

2 Plane the rail in both directions. The plane will chatter as it crosses the end grain, then begin shaving smoothly as it reaches the stile. The result at the rail will be somewhat rough but sandable.

Cutting a door

1 Cut an interior door bottom ½ inch or so above the flooring or threshold. Mark the cutting line, then scribe about 1/16 inch above the cutline with a utility knife. This is especially important when cutting across the grain or cutting a plywood veneer.

2 Start the cut with a square as a guide. Stop the saw after cutting 3 or 4 inches. Remove the square and push a straightedge against the base of the saw.

3 Clamp the straightedge at one end. Measure to be sure the circular saw will cut along the cutting line—1/16 inch below the knife line.

WHAT IF...
The door is hollow core?

Hollow-core doors are reinforced with solid edge pieces for attaching hardware and to allow slight trimming. If you cut past the solid piece, you will expose the door's hollow core.

If you do cut into the hollow part of the door, save the edge piece. Cut the facings off the edge piece with a tablesaw to make it the right thickness for reinserting in the door. If you have no tablesaw, use a hammer and chisel to cut off the facings.

Glue and clamp the edging between the two door faces. Allow the glue to dry before hanging the door.

4 Set the circular saw's blade about ¼ inch deeper than the thickness of the door. Make the cut, holding the saw's baseplate against the guide.

5 Use a sanding block to smooth the cut edge and slightly round the corners.

STANLEY PRO TIP:

Straighten a warped door

If you have a door that is warped but would be difficult to match for replacement, you may be able to straighten it. Rest both ends of the door on sawhorses and place weights in the center. Every day or two remove the weights and check with a straightedge.

Extending a door

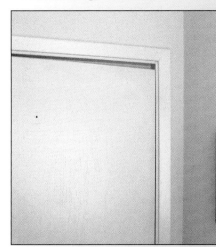

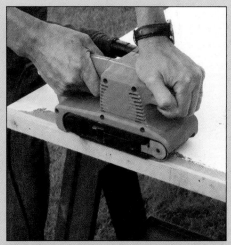

1 In an older home with an out-of-square door frame, the top of a door may be out of parallel with the top of the frame. Measure the distance between the top of the door and the frame; subtract ⅛ inch.

2 For an interior door 1⅜ inch thick, rip the extension piece from 2× lumber (which is 1½ inches thick). Cut using a circular saw or a tablesaw. For an exterior door, rip stock to the thickness of the door to cut the piece.

3 Apply wood glue to the top of the door. Attach the extension piece by drilling pilot holes and driving finishing nails or screws. Plane or power-sand the piece on both sides so it is flush with the door. Fill the joint with wood putty and sand again before painting.

REPLACING A SILL AND THRESHOLD

An exterior threshold takes a lot of abuse from foot traffic and weather, and it must be in good shape to keep the weather out. It can be replaced with a wood or metal threshold, either of which is available with a rubber gasket for sealing out the cold.

There is usually a sill below an exterior threshold. If the threshold is rotted, the sill probably is also. The sill is beveled on one side to drain water away from the house. Replace a sill using sill stock that has the same profile (shape) as the old sill. It fits tightly between wall studs and under the jambs and casing, so it has to be cut before it can be removed.

You may want to replace an interior threshold because the old one is ugly or because new flooring on one side of the doorway calls for it. An interior threshold simply rests on the floor with no sill under it.

PRESTART CHECKLIST

☐ **TIME**
2 or 3 hours

☐ **TOOLS**
Circular saw or reciprocating saw, saber saw, hammer, chisel, nail set, tape measure, square, drill

☐ **SKILLS**
Basic carpentry skills

☐ **PREP**
Protect the floor with a drop cloth.

☐ **MATERIALS**
New threshold and/or sill stock, flooring adhesive, galvanized finishing nails, caulk

Replacing a threshold

1 The threshold usually fits below the stops and against the jambs. To remove one use a nail set and hammer to poke the nails all the way through. Then tap the threshold out using a hammer and a block of wood.

2 Use the old threshold as a template to mark for cutting the new one.

THRESHOLD AND SILL CONFIGURATIONS

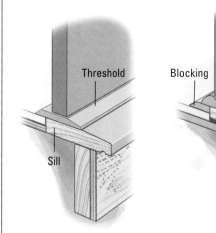

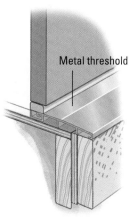

A threshold (also called a saddle) is positioned directly under the door. In some cases (above) it rests on top of a sill, which extends outward.

Or it may rest partly on the sill and partly on a piece of blocking (above).

In some newer homes there is no sill; instead a wide metal threshold extends outward to do the job of the sill (above).

3 Test the fit of the new threshold. Apply flooring adhesive to the floor, slip the threshold into place, drill pilot holes, and drive 10d casing nails to secure it. Fill the nail holes with exterior wood putty.

WHAT IF...
You are installing a metal threshold?

With a metal threshold it is usually easier to cut the stop moldings to fit around the threshold. Cut the sill with a hacksaw. Use a hammer and chisel to cut through the stops.

STANLEY PRO TIP

Install a sill cover

You can protect and liven up a sill with a metal sill cover, which wraps around the front of the sill. Cut it with a hacksaw. Install a cover alone, or purchase a cover and sill combination.

Replacing a sill

1 Because it is nailed under the jambs, you will have to cut a sill into pieces before removing it. Cut out a large middle section, then chisel or pry out the smaller sections at the sides.

2 If the old sill pieces are intact, assemble them on top of the new sill stock and use them as a template. However, measure to be sure the overall length is correct.

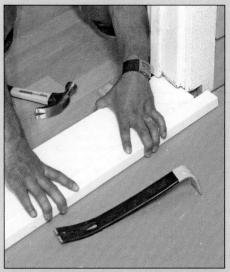

3 Tap in the new sill to be sure it fits. Apply flooring adhesive and install the new sill with 12d casing nails.

STORM DOOR REPAIRS

Storm doors are often made with flimsy parts, including the latch, hinge, and closer. Fortunately these parts are easy to replace. However, you may find it worthwhile to replace the entire storm door with a more substantial and weather-resistant one if it has several problems (see pages 176–177).

Most parts can be found at a home center. If you do not find the part you need, try searching Internet sources.

PRESTART CHECKLIST

☐ **TIME**
An hour or so for most repairs

☐ **TOOLS**
Screwdriver, drill, pliers

☐ **SKILLS**
Basic mechanical skills

☐ **PREP**
Check the door for binding and other obstructions that could be causing problems.

☐ **MATERIALS**
Replacement parts to match, spray lubricant

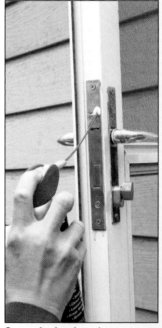

Spray the latch and any moving parts—including where panes slide—with lubricant to keep them in smooth working order.

Closers lose their dampening power over time. To install a replacement closer, use a drill with a screwdriver bit to attach the jamb-side bracket, then the screws that hold the closer to the door.

Adjust a closer to the correct tension by turning the adjustment screw at the end of the cylinder.

Try driving longer screws if the long piano-type hinge comes loose. You may need to drill pilot holes and drive them at an angle so they catch solid wood.

A wind chain keeps the door from blowing wide open, which can damage the hinge. It installs easily with a few screws.

SLIDING PATIO DOOR REPAIRS

The heavy panels of a patio door glide on rollers at the bottom; the top track is a guide only. If a door is difficult to slide, first vacuum out the track, which collects debris easily. Avoid applying lubricant to the track; it will only attract more dust and dirt. If the door still won't glide, you may need to adjust or replace the rollers.

Patio screen doors are easily bent and damaged. It is sometimes best to replace one rather than going to the trouble of trying to fix it.

PRESTART CHECKLIST

☐ **TIME**
An hour or less for most repairs

☐ **TOOLS**
Screwdriver, hammer, pliers

☐ **SKILLS**
Basic mechanical skills

☐ **PREP**
Clean the upper and lower tracks for both the patio door and screen door.

☐ **MATERIALS**
New roller or other part as needed, small block of wood

To remove a patio door, slide it to the center of the opening. With a helper lift the door up, then swing the bottom out. If the second door is fixed in place, remove any brackets and remove it the same way.

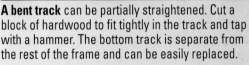

A bent track can be partially straightened. Cut a block of hardwood to fit tightly in the track and tap with a hammer. The bottom track is separate from the rest of the frame and can be easily replaced.

A door that's difficult to slide may need to be adjusted upward or downward at either end. The adjusting screws may be at the bottom face of the door or at the ends.

If the rollers are stuck, remove the door, lay it on its side, remove the adjusting screw, and pry out the roller assembly. If cleaning the unit does not restore smooth operation, replace it.

A screen roller may be attached with a screw or with a pin that can be pulled out with a screwdriver or long-nose pliers. Buy an exact replacement and install it.

REPAIRING BIFOLD AND SLIDING DOORS

Most sliding closet doors hang by rollers from a track above. Bifold doors are anchored at the bottom and top of one side. On the opposite side a guide pin slides through a top channel. Parts for these doors are readily available at home centers, hardware stores, or online.

If you have a sliding closet door that glides on a bottom track, clean the track with a damp cloth to ensure smooth gliding. Lubricate the rollers but not the track, because lubricant will act as a magnet for dust. Remove a door by lifting and tilting the bottom out. If a roller is stuck, unscrew and remove it. If cleaning does not solve the problem, replace the roller unit.

PRESTART CHECKLIST

☐ **TIME**
An hour or less for most repairs, once you have the parts in hand

☐ **TOOLS**
Screwdriver, adjustable wrench, pliers, drill

☐ **SKILLS**
Using basic carpentry tools

☐ **PREP**
Clear the area and make sure there are no obstructions hindering door operation.

☐ **MATERIALS**
Closet door parts, which come with mounting screws and other hardware

Fixing bifolds

Bifold doors should be parallel with the frame and each other when there are double bifolds in an opening. A bifold should close snugly but not too tightly. To adjust the door's position at the bottom, simply lift at the bottom and move the pin over to another position on the bracket.

To adjust the top position, partially open the door. Loosen the bracket's screw, slide the door over, and tighten the screw.

HOW A BIFOLD WORKS

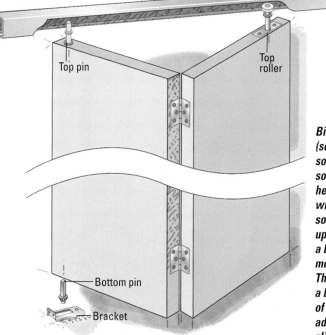

Top pin

Top roller

Bottom pin

Bracket

Bifold doors are light (some are louvered and some are hollow-core), so the hardware is not heavy-duty. A top pin, which is spring-loaded so you can lift the door up and out, inserts into a bracket that can be moved to the left or right. The bottom pin rests in a bracket with a number of setting points for easy adjustment. The top roller slides through a track.

To adjust a bifold's height, use an adjustable wrench, a pair of pliers, or the wrench that comes with the hardware. Twist the nut surrounding the pin to raise or lower the door.

If the bracket is too low (or sunk below carpeting), remove the door and the bracket. Cut a shim to fit under the bracket and reinstall the bracket.

Repair parts are easily installed; some simply push into holes, while others attach with a screw or two. If a pin or roller hole is enlarged or the door is cracked, a replacement part may not anchor securely. Buy a repair part with a flange that can be screwed to either side of the hole. If the door is badly damaged, replace it.

Adjusting sliders

To adjust the height of a hanging slider, loosen the adjusting screws on a roller bracket, move the door up or down, and retighten the screws. If your roller bracket is not adjustable, buy replacement brackets.

The doors slide through a bottom guide on the floor. If the guide is out of alignment, adjust the guide and drive longer screws. If the guide is not high enough to capture the doors, place a small shim under the guide.

To remove a hanging closet door, remove the guide. Look for access slots on the track. Slide the rollers to the slots, lift the door, and tilt the bottom out.

REPAIRING OLD LATCHES

An older interior or exterior door, and some newer high-end exterior doors, may have a mortise latch. These fit into rectangular holes (mortises) in the edge of the door. In many cases the mortise latch assembly includes a key-operated dead bolt.

If the latch does not operate smoothly, scrape away any paint buildup. (The latch itself should not be painted, though it often is.) Dig out any debris that may be holding the latch bolt. Spray a bit of graphite or silicone lubricant around the latch bolt. If these measures do not work, remove the unit and inspect it.

Repair parts or a replacement unit may not be available at a hardware store or home center. Renovation supply dealers and locksmiths may have them, or you can search Internet sources.

PRESTART CHECKLIST

☐ **TIME**
Less than an hour for repairs, but finding replacement parts may be difficult

☐ **TOOLS**
Screwdriver, pliers, vacuum or canned air

☐ **SKILLS**
Some mechanical aptitude

☐ **PREP**
Place a drop cloth on the floor below the door.

☐ **MATERIALS**
Spray lubricant, replacement parts as needed

To remove a mortise lock, remove both knobs and the shaft. (Usually you loosen a setscrew on one of the knobs, then pull it off. Some knobs screw onto the shaft.) Remove the two lock retaining screws and pry the mortise latch out.

Place the latch on a worktable. Unscrew one or two screws and carefully remove the cover. Study the parts and how they go together so you can replace them correctly.

If you see a broken part—usually a spring or an arm that connects to the latch bolt—remove it and try to find a replacement part. It may be easier to buy a whole new unit.

Vacuum away dust or clean the lock with canned air. Lightly spray with silicone lubricant or graphite (not oil; it gums up), then replace the cover. Test and then reinstall the lock.

CHOOSING REPLACEMENT LOCKS

You have plenty of options when it comes to choosing a lock. A home center provides an array of possibilities. If you want more options, including high-end locks, check with locksmiths and online sources.

Avoid inexpensive brass-plated locks. The plating often starts to wear away after a year or so and is easily scratched. Solid brass is a good option, as is chrome or nickel.

For increased security spend a bit more for a dead-bolt lock that has a security strike box and plate. This system ensures that an intruder will not be able to pry open the door when it is locked.

If you are replacing an existing lock, be sure the new one will fit into the old hole. Most dead-bolt holes are $2^1/_8$ inches in diameter, but some are only $1^1/_2$ inches. Also be sure that the backset—the distance from the edge of the door to the center of the hole—is the same. Most units can be adjusted to fit a $2^3/_8$-inch or $2^3/_4$-inch backset (the standard dimensions).

WHAT IF...
You want extra security?

A door reinforcer adds an extra measure of security, strengthening the

A single-key dead bolt has a key on the outside and a turn knob on the inside. This is the most common type because it allows easy exit during an emergency. However, if the door has a window near the dead bolt, an intruder could break the glass and reach the knob.

A double-key dead bolt offers the greatest security if the door has a glass pane, but fire safety codes often do not allow it because family members may be trapped inside during an emergency. One solution is to hang a key on a chain near the door.

Older rim locks, sometimes called night latches, were easy to pry open, but newer ones offer greater security. The rim lock mounts on the face of the door.

A dead bolt should have at least a 1-inch throw—the distance the bolt extends into the door frame. A unit with a security box and strike plate, shown above, virtually eliminates the possibility of kick-ins.

INSTALLING A LOCKSET

If you are replacing a dead bolt or handle, simply insert the new parts into the existing holes (steps 6 and 7). Before installing check that the new dead bolt will fit in the hole and that the existing mortises for the latch and the strike are not too large. (It's easy to enlarge a mortise, but it's difficult to fill in a too-large mortise so it is not noticeable.) You may need to buy a separate, larger strike plate.

If you buy a unit with a security box and strike plate, you may need to widen and deepen the strike hole, and perhaps enlarge the strike's mortise as well.

The door frame should be in good shape. If the dead bolt slides into the jamb only, an intruder will be able to kick the door in. A bolt that slides into the stud will be much more secure.

PRESTART CHECKLIST

☐ **TIME**
1 or 2 hours to install a new lockset or dead bolt

☐ **TOOLS**
Drill, hole saw and spade bit of the correct sizes, hammer, chisel, screwdriver, awl

☐ **SKILLS**
Accurate measuring and drilling

☐ **PREP**
Place a drop cloth on the floor under the door.

☐ **MATERIALS**
Lockset or dead bolt with accompanying hardware

1 Determine the best height for the lock (see below). The lock comes with a paper template. Fold the template and tape it to the door. Select a 2⅜-inch or 2¾-inch backset. Use an awl or sharp nail to poke a small hole at the center of the cylinder hole on the face of the door and the latch hole on the edge of the door.

2 Insert the tip of the hole saw's guide bit into the awl hole. Drill, taking care to hold the bit level and at a right angle to the door. (Guides are available; see below.) Stop when the guide bit pokes through the other side. Drill from the other side to complete the hole.

WHERE TO POSITION LOCKSET, DEAD BOLT

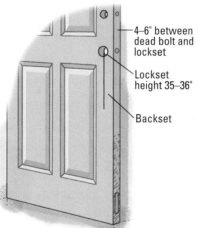

4–6" between dead bolt and lockset

Lockset height 35–36"

Backset

When you drill holes for a new dead bolt or lockset in a hollow-core door or a door filled with particleboard or high-density foam, be sure the holes will be drilled through the solid wood lock block in the door. Place the handle where it is comfortable to reach, and position the center of the dead bolt hole at least 4 inches from the center of the handle's hole.

 **STANLEY** PRO TIP

Installation kit

A lock and dead-bolt installation kit includes the hole saw and the spade bit you will need. Some kits have plastic guides that make it easy to drill holes that are level and at right angles to the door.

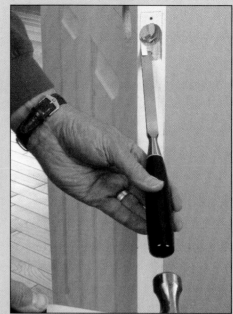

3 Switch to a spade bit and drill the latch hole through the edge of the door, using the awl hole as a guide. Drill all the way into the cylinder hole. Some locks call for continuing to drill on the other side of the cylinder hole. Clean away sawdust.

4 Insert the latch into the latch hole and temporarily anchor it with screws, with the bolt centered in the hole and the latch's plate centered in the door edge. Mark with a knife for cutting the mortise around the plate.

5 Use a hammer and a sharp chisel to cut a mortise in the edge of the door. First use the chisel to cut the lines about ¼ inch deep. Then chisel from the hole outward.

6 Insert the latch into the mortise and check that the plate will be flush with the door edge. You may need to remove the latch and chisel a bit more. If the plate is set too deep, insert small shims. Drill pilot holes and drive screws to attach the latch.

7 Insert the inside portion of the lockset—the one that has a tab that fits through the latch—until it rests flush against the door. Insert the other portion and drive screws to attach the two. This can sometimes be tricky; have a helper hold the inside portion while you drive the screws.

STANLEY PRO TIP

Adding a metal reinforcement

To add a door reinforcement, remove the dead-bolt handle and faceplate and simply slip the metal piece over the door edge. Reinstall the dead-bolt handle and drive the small screws.

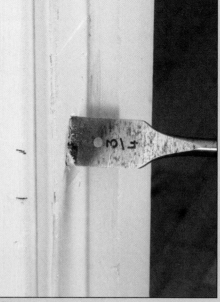

8 Slide the latch bolt partway out and gently close the door. Mark the edge of the jamb for the vertical center of the bolt. Use a square to transfer this height to the inside face of the jamb, and mark for the horizontal center, which is half the thickness of the door.

9 If you are installing a standard bolt, you need drill only one hole. To install a security strike box, mark the outline of the box and drill two holes, one above and one below the mark.

10 For a security box, chisel out the area to create a rectangular hole.

Installing a peephole

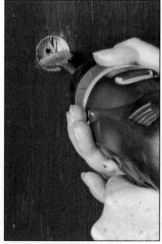

1 Center the peephole about 65 inches above the floor. Drill a hole with a spade or a Forstner bit, stopping just when the point breaks through the other side.

2 Finish the hole from the opposite side of the door. Hold the drill back from pushing through; it is easy to splinter the other side.

3 Push the lens end of the peephole into the hole on the outside of the door.

4 Finish the installation by screwing the inner ring in place.

11 Close the door and check that the bolt slides easily into the hole. Temporarily attach the strike plate and mark for the mortise with a knife.

12 Chisel the mortise as in step 5, but make it shallower. Insert the strike box (if any) and secure it with screws. Close the door and test that the latch slides easily into the hole.

13 Attach the strike plate, drill pilot holes, and drive the mounting screws.

14 Test the lock again. If the bolt does not slide easily into the strike, try tapping the strike with a hammer and screwdriver. Or you may need to file or move the plate (see page 126).

STANLEY. PRO TIP

Securing the strike

The strike plate (and the security strike box, if you have one) should be securely attached. Short screws driven only into the jamb provide limited strength; it's much stronger to drive screws into a stud. You may be able to replace the short screws with long screws that reach the stud. If there is a wide gap between the jamb and the stud, remove the casing and slip a piece of plywood between the jamb and the stud, taking care not to bow the jamb. Secure the plywood to the stud with angle-driven screws and attach the strike plate with screws driven through the plywood into the stud.

WHAT IF...
Your hinge pins are outside?

If your door's hinge pins are exposed on the outside, an intruder can remove the pin to easily open the door. Install a security hinge pin, which makes it impossible to remove the door even with the hinge pin removed.

SPRUCING UP AN ENTRY DOOR WITH TRIM

Installing decorative trim around an entry door—whether old or newly installed—is a quick way to give your house a facelift. With the advent of urethane foam molding, there is now a wide range of affordable molding styles to choose from.

Urethane foam trim is light, paintable, easy to cut, and will never rot—ideal for exterior trim. The trim shown here can be purchased at a home center. For a larger selection, check online sources. You may need to measure your door and order the header—the horizontal piece at the top—at a certain length. The casing (the vertical pieces that replace the brick molding) can be cut to length.

PRESTART CHECKLIST

☐ **TIME**
Most of a day to install decorative trim around an entry door

☐ **TOOLS**
Tape measure, hammer, flat pry bar, circular saw, clamps, utility knife, nail set, caulk gun, putty knife, sanding block

☐ **SKILLS**
Measuring, cutting, fastening

☐ **PREP**
Measure the doorway and buy the trim pieces. Protect the area with a drop cloth.

☐ **MATERIALS**
Urethane foam moldings to fit your doorway, 6d and 10d casing nails, adhesive recommended for your moldings, exterior caulk, exterior putty

1 Using a flat pry bar, carefully remove the brick molding from around the door. Be careful not to dent the siding or the jambs; using a scrap of wood as a fulcrum helps.

2 Scrape away any accumulated paint or putty from the jamb. If the reveal line is not clearly visible along the jamb edge, scribe a reveal line (see page 100). If needed, seal and insulate the gap between the jamb and the framing with non-expanding spray foam insulation.

AN ENTRYWAY UPGRADE

A crisply trimmed doorway (perhaps coupled with a new paint job) can make your home an inviting destination.

3 To establish the width of the header (the piece above the door), hold each piece of casing in place and mark along its outside edge. Measure between the marks. The header looks best if it extends beyond the casing; add twice the thickness of the header to the overall length and mark for cutting.

4 Miter the ends of the header. Urethane foam cuts as easily as wood, but if the saw blade binds and overheats, a hard crust will build up. If this happens, pare off the crust with a utility knife.

5 To assure that the header will stand proud of the casing, glue in place urethane parting stop along the inside of the top and bottom of the header. Cut small mitered pieces of the header to create a return (see page 101). Glue and tape both pieces in place.

6 Cut the casing to length. Position each piece of casing and check that it meets against the reveal line. Drill pilot holes and attach the casing with 6d casing nails driven into the jambs and 10d nails driven into the sheathing and studs.

7 Set the header in place and center it so it extends equally beyond each piece of casing. Drill pilot holes and fasten it as you did the casing.

8 Set the nails and fill with exterior wood filler. Sand the filler when it is dry. Apply exterior-grade caulking all around where the molding meets the siding.

WEATHERSTRIPPING A DOOR

A door that is not well sealed allows a lot of heat to escape from the house through gaps around the sides and bottom. A variety of easy-to-install weatherstripping products can help solve the problem. A storm door (pages 176–177) will also help reduce heat loss and energy costs.

A typical door opens and closes thousands of times per year, so choose durable weatherstripping products that can be attached securely. Vinyl V-strip and self-stick foam, for instance, are suitable for a window (see pages 60–61) but will probably not last on a door.

By using a combination of products, you can double the protection. For instance, seal a door along the sides and top by installing spring bronze for the edges of the door and outside gasket weatherstripping against the door's face on the outside. Weatherproof the bottom using a sweep on the door's inside face and a weatherstripping threshold or a door shoe on the bottom edge.

PRESTART CHECKLIST

☐ **TIME**
About an hour for most weatherstripping applications

☐ **TOOLS**
Tape measure, knife, tin snips, hacksaw, drill, screwdriver, hammer, putty knife

☐ **SKILLS**
Measuring and cutting, driving screws and nails

☐ **PREP**
Make any needed repairs to the door and its frame (see pages 122–131).

☐ **MATERIALS**
Door weatherstripping products, which come with mounting screws or nails

Door sweep

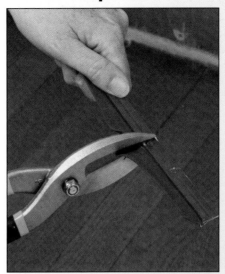

1 The quickest and easiest way to seal a leaky door bottom is with a sweep. Use tin snips or a hacksaw to cut the sweep to the full width of the door bottom.

2 Close the door. Hold the sweep against the threshold but not so tight that it would make the door difficult to close. Drill pilot holes through the center of the holes and attach the sweep with screws. Test by opening and closing the door. Adjust the sweep up or down as needed.

STANLEY PRO TIP

Problem-solver sweeps

Got a serious case of "gap-itis" beneath your door? A heavy-duty sweep (top) can seal up to ¾-inch of gap. Or perhaps no overhang protects your door? Seal it with a drip-cap door sweep (center). If your threshold is rough or misshapen, a brush sweep (bottom) may stop the gap better than vinyl or reinforced rubber.

WHAT IF...
You need to replace a gasket?

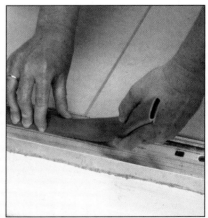

If you have a metal threshold with a rubber gasket, replace the gasket as soon as you see signs of wear. Use a putty knife to pry out the old gasket and to press the new one into the threshold's channel.

Door shoe

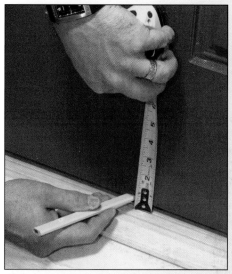

1 A door shoe seals more effectively than a sweep. If there is already enough room between the door's bottom and the threshold, simply cut and install the shoe (next step). If there is not enough room, measure and cut the door as needed (see pages 128–129).

2 Slip the door shoe onto the door bottom and close the door. Adjust the shoe's position so its rubber gasket seals against the threshold. Drill pilot holes and drive screws to attach.

WHAT IF...
Kerf-in weatherstripping

If you have a metal door with a special kerf (thin groove) along the jamb, it is a simple matter to replace worn weatherstripping. Buy "magnetic kerf-in weatherstripping" and press it into the kerf using a putty knife.

Sealing the edges and top

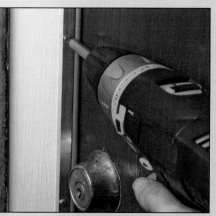

To seal along the door's edge on the sides and top, spring bronze is the best product. Measure carefully and use tin snips to cut the pieces to fit. At the latch you may be able to cut a notch or you may need to cut a small piece that goes behind the latch. Position the pieces carefully and drive small nails to attach. If the door fits tightly, you may need to do some planing (page 127).

To seal the door's sides and top from the outside, close the door. Use tin snips to cut pieces of metal outside gasket weatherstripping. Press lightly against the door and drive screws or nails to attach.

Install wood-and-rubber outside gasket weatherstripping in the same way. Cut with a saw or tin snips and drive nails to attach.

INSTALLING DOORS

Whether you want to replace an existing door or cut a hole in a wall and install a new doorway, there is a wide range of door styles and types to choose from. See pages 18–23 to peruse the various types and styles of doors, as well as the choices of materials.

This chapter shows how to frame for and install interior and exterior doors of all types. Before you replace a door with another of the same type, consider other possibilities. For instance, you may be able to replace a standard exterior door with a larger patio door. A pocket door can sometimes replace a regular interior door and save space at the same time; a 3-foot-wide door to a laundry room can often be widened to 6 feet or so with bifold or sliding doors.

The advantage of prehungs

If you buy a simple door unattached to jambs, you will face several difficult chores. You may need to cut the door to fit the existing doorjambs, which can be difficult if the jambs are not square. You will also need to bore holes for the lockset and chisel mortises for the hinges. These tasks are not easy. Errors could cause you to ruin a door.

Those are some of the reasons why even expert carpenters prefer prehung doors. A prehung door has factory-installed hinges and precisely drilled holes, ensuring that the door will fit correctly and close easily and tightly. Even if your doorway is in relatively good shape, it is often better to remove the existing casing and jambs and install a prehung unit.

CHAPTER PREVIEW

Hanging an old door in a new jamb
page 148

Fitting a new door to an old opening
page 150

Framing an interior doorway
page 152

Installing a prehung door
page 156

Framing for closet doors
page 160

Installing bypass and bifold doors
page 162

Customizing standard prehungs
For a unique entryway consider upgrading a standard door. This plain fiberglass exterior prehung gets updated with a paint job and a new porthole window. The result: a one-of-a-kind entry.

Installing a pocket door
page 164

Installing door and window casing
page 166

Framing for a new exterior door
page 168

Installing a storm door
page 176

Installing a patio door
page 178

Garage door maintenance and weatherstripping
page 184

HANGING AN OLD DOOR IN A NEW JAMB

If you want to keep an old door but the old jambs are damaged or you want to install an old door in new construction, purchase a door frame, sometimes called a jamb kit, at a lumberyard or home center. The kit consists of three pieces of lumber ⁹/₁₆ inch thick and 4³/₈ inches wide. The two side jambs are milled across the top to receive the third piece, the head jamb.

The first step is to make the door fit the opening or vice versa. A properly sized door is about 2¼ inches narrower than the rough opening and 1 inch shorter than the distance from the header to the finished floor. If you have to cut a panel door a significant amount in width, trim from both edges to keep the stiles symmetrical. Try not to cut hollow-core doors beyond the solid edges. If you have to cut into the hollow area, save the solid edges and glue them back onto the door to reinforce it.

PRESTART CHECKLIST

☐ **TIME**
About 1 to 3 hours

☐ **TOOLS**
Table saw, circular saw, router, tape measure, layout square, chisels, drill/driver, utility knife

☐ **SKILLS**
Accurate measuring and laying out, cutting with power saws, routing hinge mortises, trimming with a chisel, driving screws

☐ **PREP**
Check that the rough door opening is square and the used door is square and flat.

☐ **MATERIALS**
Jamb kit, 2½-inch screws, doorstop molding

1 Hook the tape measure into the side jamb rabbets or dadoes and measure down a distance equal to the length of the door. Add ¾ inch clearance for an interior door or ¼ inch for an exterior door, plus the thickness of any flooring that will be added later. Cut the jambs to this length.

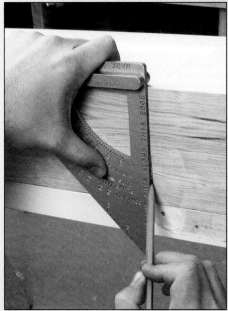

2 Hold the hinge jamb alongside the edge of the door and lay out the hinge locations on the jamb. The top of the door should be just slightly more than ¹/₁₆ inch below the edge of the rabbet or dado. Mark the mortise locations with a sharp pencil.

WHAT IF...
The door needs new hinge mortises?

If a used door must be trimmed to size, cut or plane the edge to remove the old mortises. This prevents having to find hinges to match the old mortises.

Most doors require three hinges (hollow-core doors need only two). If neither the door nor the jamb has mortises, center the middle hinge and place the other hinges about 6 inches from the top and bottom of the door.

Cut the mortises in the door first. You can cut them with a router or a chisel. Clamp some 2×4 scraps on both sides of the door to keep the router from tipping. To make the job easier, buy a hinge mortise template for routing (page 150). Routed mortises have rounded corners; square them with a chisel if your hinges have square corners. Transfer the locations to the jamb.

3 Scribe the hinge leaf outline onto the door edge with a sharp utility knife. Set a ½-inch straight router bit slightly deeper than the hinge leaf thickness. Rout close to the scribe lines. Finetune the mortise with a chisel.

4 Cut the head jamb to a length equal to the door width plus the combined rabbet or dado depth plus slightly more than ⅛ inch. Screw the door frame together by drilling pilot holes and driving 2½-inch screws. Attach the hinges to the jamb and the door.

5 Hang the door as you would a prehung unit. Check its fit in the opening before securing the jamb. Plane the strike-side edge of the door if necessary. Cut the stop moldings and install them (page 158).

WHAT IF...
You don't have a router?

1 You can cut hinge mortises by hand with a chisel. Hold the hinge in place and scribe around it with a utility knife. Mark the depth of the mortise on the edge of the jamb with your knife, using a combination square as a guide. Make the mortise slightly deeper than the thickness of the hinge leaf.

2 Sharpen a chisel—one that's 1 inch to 1½ inches wide is best. Cut down close to the mortise depth around the mortise.

3 Once you have defined the outline of the mortise, pare away the wood until the mortise is cut to its full depth. Keep the bottom of the mortise as flat as possible so the hinge will seat evenly.

FITTING A NEW DOOR TO AN OLD OPENING

If an existing door is damaged or worn, you can put a new door into the doorway. Often the easiest way is to remove the existing jambs and casing and install a prehung door. However, if the doorway is square or if the existing trim is difficult to replace, you can keep the doorway and replace the door.

Unless your house is very old, you'll have little problem finding doors to fit. The most common door height is 80 inches, although most are available 78 inches tall as well. Common interior door widths are 24, 28, 30, 32, and 36 inches. Height and width are often stated in feet and inches: 2-6 for 30 inches or 3-0 for 36 inches, for instance.

Check that the doorway is square. If not, scribe and plane the door. If the doorway is well out of square, remove the casing, cut through the nails holding the jambs, and reattach the jambs so they are square.

PRESTART CHECKLIST

☐ **TIME**
About 3 to 4 hours

☐ **TOOLS**
Tape measure, block plane, square, router, chisels, drill/driver, 2⅛-inch hole saw, 1-inch spade bit, utility knife

☐ **SKILLS**
Measuring and laying out, planing, cutting mortises, drilling

☐ **PREP**
Remove the old door, check the opening for square, and acquire new hardware if necessary.

☐ **MATERIALS**
New door, new hardware (if needed), shims, matchbooks

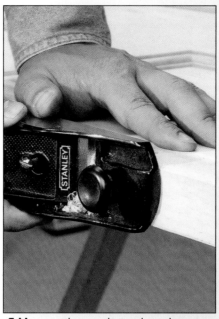

1 Measure the opening and purchase a door that fits. If you have to trim the door, take an equal amount off each side. Plane a slight bevel (about 5 degrees) on the strike side of the door to ease opening and closing.

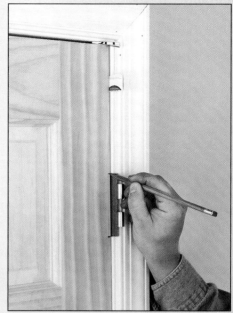

2 Check the door fit. Ideally there should be a gap of about ⅛ inch at the top and along each side, and about ⅜ inch at the bottom. Use cardboard spacers or folded matchbooks (four thicknesses equals about ¹⁄₁₆ inch) along with shims underneath to maintain the spacing. Mark the mortise locations and cut the mortises as described on pages 148–149.

STANLEY PRO TIP: **Mortising jigs**

If you have more than one or two doors to hang, consider investing in a hinge-mortising jig, which is a template for guiding a router to cut perfect mortises for hinges. Several models are available. The simplest (and least expensive) ones cut one mortise at a time, leaving the placement of the matching mortise up to you. More complex jigs come with multiple templates that will position matching mortises on the jamb and door edge.

Most hinge-mortising jigs work with a router equipped with a template guide. The guide could be a roller bearing on the bit, as shown here, or a metal collar attached to the router's base that surrounds the bit and runs along the mortise template.

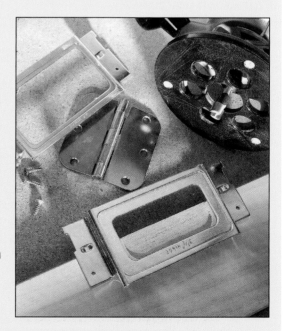

3 Hang the door. New locksets come with a template to help you locate where to drill holes. If you are reusing a lockset, extend a line across the face of the door with your square, making sure it is centered on the strike plate. Measure the lockset to determine the distance the hole should be from the edge of the door. Drill a 2⅛-inch hole through the door with a hole saw.

4 For the bolt, drill a 1-inch hole through the edge of the door with a spade bit. Make sure the hole is centered between the front and back door faces and aligned with the center of the strike plate.

5 Insert the bolt into the hole in the door's edge. Align the bolt plate with the edges of the door and trace around it with a utility knife. Remove the bolt and cut away the wood inside the outline to create a mortise for the plate. When finished the plate should lie slightly below the surface.

WHAT IF...
There are no hinge mortises in the opening?

Some houses have openings that are trimmed out like a doorway with jambs and casings but have no door. These might be found, for example, between a kitchen and dining room or a den and a hallway. If you decide to add a door, you'll have to cut mortises in the jambs to hang the door and install stop molding.

If the opening is finished only with drywall, you may be able to treat it as you would a rough opening and install a prehung door. If the rough opening was framed to a standard size and ½-inch drywall was used, check to see if the opening is square. If it is you can nail the door frame directly against the drywall opening. Otherwise you'll need to remove the corner bead and the drywall from the jamb and header faces to make room for shims.

1 Check carefully for nails, then lay out the hinge mortises on the jamb. Rout close to the layout lines. Finish the mortises with a sharp chisel. Hold the door in the opening with shims and transfer the marks.

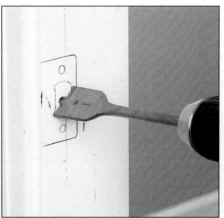

2 After the door is hung and the lockset installed, rub a little lipstick on the bolt to mark the jamb for the strike plate. Using a spade bit, drill a 1-inch hole for the bolt; mortise the strike plate into the jamb with a chisel.

FRAMING AN INTERIOR DOORWAY

It is easier to build a wall flat on the floor if you have the space. Otherwise attach a top plate to the ceiling and use a level or plumb bob to position the bottom plate on the floor. Then cut individual studs and attach them with angle-driven screws or nails.

Select the straightest studs you can find for framing; you will avoid problems later. Check each stud for a crown—a slight curve along its length—and install all the studs with the crowns facing the same direction.

Build the wall with a bottom plate running across the doorway. This keeps the entire wall in one plane as you install it. Then you can cut the bottom plate out after the wall is installed. To make it easier to remove the bottom plate under the door, cut most of the way through it in the correct places with a circular saw.

PRESTART CHECKLIST

☐ **TIME**
About 2 hours

☐ **TOOLS**
Tape measure, layout square, circular saw, handsaw, hammer, level

☐ **SKILLS**
Measuring and marking, crosscutting, driving nails

☐ **PREP**
Measure the length of the wall and determine the correct rough opening for the door.

☐ **MATERIALS**
2×4s, 16d nails, 10d nails, 8d nails

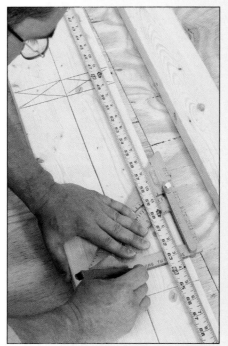

1 Lay out the positions of the studs. Space the studs 16 inches on center—every multiple of 16 inches falls in the center of a stud. To do this, mark for each stud ¾ inch short of the multiple of 16 inches. Mark for the opening's jack stud and king stud (see pages 92–93).

2 Install the regular studs and the king studs. Cut the jack studs to a length equal to the rough opening height minus 1½ inches to allow for the bottom plate. Nail the jack studs to the bottom plate with 16d nails and to the sides of the king studs with 10d nails.

Leaving room for adjustment

The rough opening is taller and wider than the assembled door jambs to allow space for the jambs plus a little extra for shimming the assembly should the opening not be exactly plumb or square.

A typical residential door is 32 inches wide and 80 inches tall, so the rough opening is 34 inches wide and 82 inches tall. Rather than rely on these dimensions, however, purchase (or at least measure) the door you will be installing before framing the opening. If you are in doubt about how big to make the opening, make it ¼ inch on the larger side. You can always shim a too-small door to fit, but a door that is too big for its opening is a nuisance to cut down. .

3 If the wall is not load-bearing, make the header from doubled 2×4s nailed together with 10d nails. Install the header with two 16d nails through each king stud. (For a header on a load-bearing wall, see pages 168–170.)

4 Nail one cripple to each king stud with 10d nails to hold the header firmly down on the jack studs. Attach them to the top plate with 16d nails. The infill cripples continue the 16-inch on-center spacing of the wall studs regardless of where the door is located. Space the infill cripples accordingly. Attach them with 16d nails through the top plate and 8d toenails into the header. Make sure the sides of the door opening are plumb. Tip the wall into place.

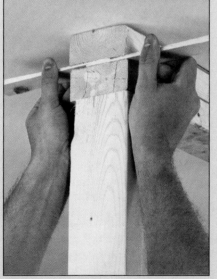

5 Attach a top plate at the ceiling. Anchor the wall by nailing up to the ceiling plate. Check the wall for plumb with a level and nail the bottom plate to the floor.

6 If there is a space between the top plate and the ceiling plate, slip a pair of shims between the two before nailing. Drive the nails through the shims to keep them from slipping out.

STANLEY PRO TIP

Need an extra set of hands?

When you are trying to tap a wall into position and get it plumb, it can be awkward to hold a level at the same time. Clamp a level to the side of one of the studs for hands-free viewing.

FRAMING WITH METAL STUDS

The traditional choice of materials for framing houses is wood. In commercial construction steel framing is the norm, largely because steel studs are inherently fire-resistant. Steel framing, however, is gradually catching on with home remodelers. It has some real advantages over wood: It is lightweight, inexpensive, and strong. In addition, it won't rot, shrink, or warp (steel framing is ideal for framing walls in a basement, where moisture can create problems).

Walls framed with steel are built in place, one piece at a time. The primary fastener is a sheet metal screw; the primary tools are a drill/driver and metal snips.

SAFETY FIRST
Protect your eyes

It's smart to wear safety goggles or safety glasses whenever you drive fasteners, but especially so when driving into concrete, which chips easily when hit.

PRESTART CHECKLIST

☐ **TIME**
About 2 to 3 hours for a 12-foot wall

☐ **TOOLS**
Tape measure, chalkline, plumb bob, drill/driver, metal snips

☐ **SKILLS**
Measuring and laying out, power-driving screws, cutting sheet metal

☐ **PREP**
Plan the wall location and measure the height of the wall in several spots.

☐ **MATERIALS**
Metal track and studs (4 studs for the first 4 feet of wall, 3 studs for every 4 feet thereafter), pan-head sheet metal screws

1 Lay out both sides of the wall on the floor with chalklines. For a concrete floor predrill ⅛-inch holes and attach the track with masonry screws. Use pan-head sheet metal screws for a wood floor.

2 Transfer the layout from the floor to the ceiling with a plumb bob (you can use a chalkline). If your wall runs parallel to the joists, install blocking to provide an anchor point. Screw the track to the joists with pan-head sheet metal screws.

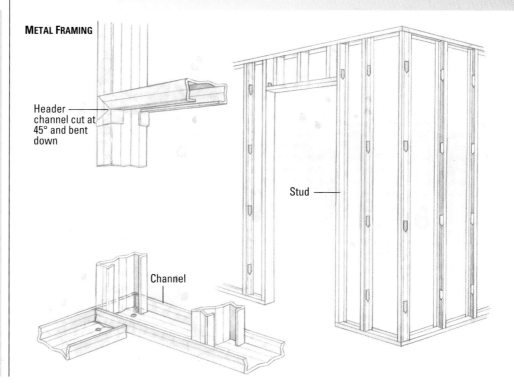

METAL FRAMING

Header channel cut at 45° and bent down

Channel

Stud

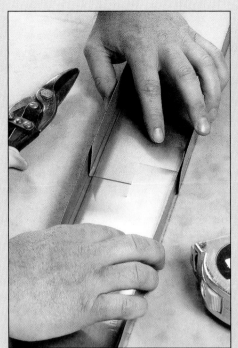

3 To splice two lengths of track together, cut a 2-inch slit in the center of one piece's web and compress opposite flanges slightly as you slide the pieces together. For corners remove the flange from one of the pieces and overlap the webs as shown in the illustration on the opposite page.

4 Lay out the stud locations on the top and bottom tracks. Cut the studs to length and stand them in the tracks. Friction will hold them in place while you check them for plumb. Fasten them with short pan-head sheet metal screws.

5 Make doorway headers from lengths of track. Cut the flanges at 45 degrees and bend down the web to form a right angle. The bent part should be about 1½ to 2 inches long. Attach the header with a single screw driven through each of the four resulting tabs.

Fastening metal framing

Metal framing requires a variety of specific screws. Panhead sheet metal screws ½ inch long are used for fastening metal pieces. These screws can also be used to attach the track to a wooden floor and ceiling joists. If the ceiling is already covered with drywall, use 1¼-inch-long screws to reach through the drywall into the joists. Drywall screws 1¼ inches long are used for attaching drywall to metal studs. Attach trim with 1½-inch (or longer) trimhead screws; their small-diameter heads countersink neatly, making it easy to fill the resulting holes. To fasten metal track to a concrete floor, use power-actuated fasteners or concrete screws. The power-actuated fasteners are fired from a nail gun you can rent. Use a No. 3 load with a ½- or ⅝-inch pin.

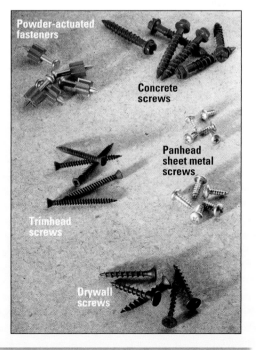

Powder-actuated fasteners

Concrete screws

Panhead sheet metal screws

Trimhead screws

Drywall screws

Add plywood blocking

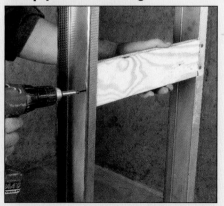

If you will be hanging cabinets or trim on a wall that's framed with metal studs, install pieces of ¾-inch plywood between the studs to provide a surface to screw into. You can insert 2×4s into headers and studs at door openings to provide a surface for attaching doorjambs.

INSTALLING A PREHUNG DOOR

A prehung unit takes a lot of the demanding precision work out of installing a door. Hinge mortises and holes for the lockset and strike are already cut. But you still need to work carefully for best results. Check that the rough opening is fairly square and plumb. As you work continually double-check the unit for square and plumb. Take the time to fix mistakes as they occur rather than hoping they will be hidden by the next step.

If you are hanging a door in an older house, keep an eye on the big picture. Before setting the nails step back and look at your work. If the wall or floor is off level or plumb, you may want to align the door frame at least a little bit out of plumb in the same direction so it blends in. For example, if the wall leans slightly, match the jamb to the wall. It won't be noticeable as long as the door doesn't lean enough to open or close by itself.

PRESTART CHECKLIST

☐ **TIME**
About 2 hours per door

☐ **TOOLS**
Level, circular saw, layout square, hammer, nail set, utility knife

☐ **SKILLS**
Cutting, driving nails, checking for plumb

☐ **PREP**
Frame the doorway and apply drywall to both sides.

☐ **MATERIALS**
Prehung door to fit the opening, shims, 16d finishing nails, 8d finishing nails

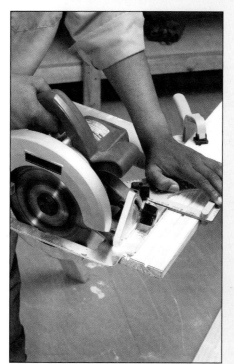

1 Tap out the hinge pins with a screwdriver and hammer; remove the door. Slip the frame into the doorway and check the head jamb for level. If it isn't level, shim under the jamb on the low side. Measure the shimmed space; cut off an equal amount from the opposite jamb.

2 Check that the jack stud on the hinge side of the opening is plumb. Also check to see if the wall leans. If the jack stud is plumb, nail the jamb directly to it with 16d finishing nails, two below each hinge and two near the center.

WHAT IF...
You are planning to install hardwood flooring or tile?

A prehung door usually has a 1¼-inch gap at the bottom of the door. This provides clearance for a carpet and pad (about 1 inch). If you plan to install hardwood floors, which are ¾ inch thick, you should cut down the jambs by ⅞ inch (¾ inch for the floor plus ⅛ inch to reduce the gap under the door). Engineered flooring is ⅜ inch thick, so cut the jambs ½ inch (⅜ inch for the floor plus ⅛ inch to reduce the gap under the door). This allows the flooring to run under the ends of the jambs. If the floor under the doorway isn't level, adjust the jambs as shown in step 1 above. Tile thicknesses vary as does the thickness of the adhesive. Check them. Allow ¼ inch between tile and door bottom.

After cutting the jambs to the right length to accommodate hardwood flooring, use a scrap of flooring (above) as a temporary spacer to help position the jambs in the doorway.

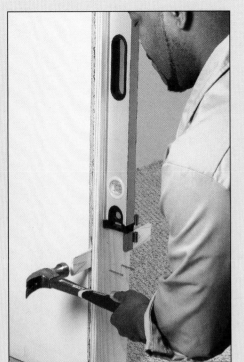

3 If the hinge-side stud is not plumb, nail the top or bottom (whichever is closer to the center of the opening). Insert shims at the opposite end to make the jamb plumb. Below the shims drive two 16d finishing nails just far enough to hold the shims and jambs in place. Adjust shims if necessary.

4 Before setting nails check that the hinge jamb is centered across the wall thickness. A typical jamb is slightly wider than the wall thickness to allow for irregularities in the drywall. If adjustment is necessary pull the nails, protecting the jamb with a scrap under the hammer.

5 Put the door back on its hinges and swing it closed. Insert shims between the jamb and the stud about halfway between the hinges. Adjust the shims until the gap between the door and jamb is equal from top to bottom. Open the door and drive two 16d finishing nails below the shims.

Dealing with doors: Which hand is which?

When ordering doors you will probably end up in a discussion about right- and left-hand doors. This can be confusing, in part because locksets and doors use the same terminology in slightly different ways.

For doors: If the hinges are on the left and you have to pull the door open, it is a left-hand door, as shown at right. If the hinges are on the right when you pull the door, it's a right-hand door.

For locksets the hand is determined from outside the room. If the door swings into the room and the hinges are on the left, the lockset is left-hand. If the door swings out of the room and the hinges are on the left, the lockset is left-hand reverse. If hinges are on the right, the lockset can similarly be right-hand or right-hand reverse.

The best way to avoid confusion is to draw

diagrams of exactly what you want; then show the diagrams to your supplier.

STANLEY PRO TIP

Check for hidden bumps

When prehung doors are assembled, the hinge screws sometimes poke through the back of the jamb. If your rough opening is tight or out of plumb, these can catch. Back them out slightly and try again.

6 The strike side of the frame is also nailed in three places: top, bottom, and middle. Insert shims and adjust so the gap between the door and the jamb is even, top to bottom. Nail the jamb in place with pairs of 16d nails driven just below the shims.

7 To get the stops in the right position, screw the strike plate to the jamb, slip the bolt into the door, and screw it in place. There is no need to install the entire lockset at this time.

8 On many prehung units the doorstops are only temporarily attached so they can be mounted permanently after the unit is in place. Pry the stops free. Close the door and hold it tightly against the strike plate. Using a playing card as a spacer, nail the stops in place while holding them against the door.

WHAT IF...
The jack stud is twisted?

One common problem you may come up against when installing a prehung door is a twisted jack stud. Even if you carefully select framing lumber and craft the wall frame accurately, it is possible for the studs to move as they adjust to conditions in the house. The result is often a door opening that isn't true. If you attach a door frame to a twisted jack stud, it will look as though the door is standing partially open; actually, the entire door frame will be protruding into the room.

You can force the frame back into the plane of the wall, but you'll risk damaging the frame. Instead, add a third shim and tap it in until the frame is square.

A twisted jack stud won't allow a door frame to stand properly in its opening.

Adding a third shim compensates for the twisted jack stud and allows the door frame to assume a proper square position.

9 If the door and jamb are to be painted, use a matchbook cover as a spacer between the door and stop as you nail the stop in place. This allows for the thickness of the paint on the various surfaces.

10 When you are satisfied with the fit of the door within the frame and the frame within the opening, drive 8d finishing nails through the jambs and shims to lock the shims in place. Cut off the shims with a utility knife or handsaw.

11 As a final step replace two of the screws in each hinge with longer screws that reach into the jack studs. The door then hangs from the jack studs, not just from the jambs.

STANLEY PRO TIP: **There's more than one way to plumb a door**

To install door frames efficiently, you need a long level. A 48-inch model is adequate, but a 72-inch level is the best tool to use. If you don't want to invest in either of these tools, there is another approach. Instead of a level you can use a plumb bob to check whether the jambs are plumb and straight. To use this method, secure the hinge-side jamb to the jack stud with three pairs of shims as described on page 157. Drive a 16d finishing nail partially into the jamb near the top (the stop will eventually cover the hole). Hang a plumb from the nail so it dangles almost to the floor. Adjust the shims until the gap between the jamb and the string is equal from top to bottom. Pin the shims in place with 8d finishing nails.

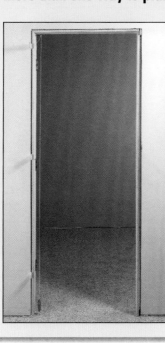

Hang a plumb bob alongside a door jamb to give yourself an immediate reference for plumbing the jamb. This simple tool eliminates the need for a long level when installing doors.

Adjust the shims behind the jamb until the distance from the jamb to the string is equal all along the length of the jamb. Add pairs of shims if necessary to compensate for a warped jamb.

FRAMING FOR CLOSET DOORS

The term "framing" here refers to installing the jambs into a rough opening for bypass or bifold doors (pages 162–163). These closet doors are not available as prehung units.

A 6-foot-wide closet opening is most common, but you can install closet doors in an opening of just about any width. Sets of bifolds are available in a variety of widths (in multiples of 2 inches) and bypass doors can be cut to any width desired. The standard height is 80 inches (the same as for an entry door). If you have an older home with 9- or 10-foot-high ceilings, this can leave you with unusable space above the doors. Either build shelves with small doors above the closet or custom-make bypass doors that are tall enough to suit your situation.

PRESTART CHECKLIST

☐ **TIME**
Once the rough framing is completed, about 3 hours to build a finish frame (jambs) for a closet

☐ **TOOLS**
Miter box or power mitersaw, circular saw, tape measure, hammer, drill, level, framing square

☐ **SKILLS**
Measuring, using a level, cutting, fastening

☐ **PREP**
Remove jambs from an existing opening, or build a new rough opening.

☐ **MATERIALS**
Jamb stock or 1× lumber the same thickness of your walls, casing, finishing nails, shims

1 If you do not already have one, build a wall for the closet, with a header above (see pages 152–155). A header that spans 6 feet should be made of 2×8s or larger, even if it is not load-bearing. Check that the opening is the correct size for the bifold or sliding doors you will install (see pages 162–163). Measure the diagonals to be sure that the opening is at least within ⅜ inch of square and ensure that the sides are plumb and the header is level.

Finish the opening by installing drywall on each side. Buy three pieces of jamb stock—two for the sides and one for the header—that are the same width as your wall's thickness. If your wall is an odd thickness, rip pieces of 1× finish-grade lumber to the correct width.

STANLEY PRO TIP: **Cutting a rabbet**

1 Rabbet joints at the corners are stronger and neater looking than simply butting two pieces of wood together. You may be able to buy jamb stock that already has rabbets. If not, mark a line ¾ inch from the end. Set a circular saw to cut ¼ to ⅜ inch deep and make a series of cuts, starting at the line.

2 Remove as much of the wood as you can by tapping gently with a hammer. Clean the joint with a wood chisel.

2 Cut the jamb sides and head to length, taking into account the depth of the rabbets in the sides. On the floor assemble the parts and measure to make sure the assembly will fit the opening and doors. Assemble with nails or drill pilot holes and drive screws.

3 Cut pieces of casing molding, making 45-degree miters at the corners. Scribe a reveal line along the edge of the jambs (see page 100), cut the casing pieces, and attach the casing to the jamb with 3d finishing nails. Check with a framing square as you work.

4 If you have covered your floor to protect it during construction, remove the covering in the doorway; it's tough to cut around the jamb and trim to remove it later.

5 Tilt the frame into the doorway. On one side check the jamb for plumb and press the casing against the wall. Tack (partially drive) several 6d finishing nails or trimhead screws to hold it in place.

6 Check the corners for square and the header for level; you may need to raise or lower the jamb on either side. Tap in shims from either side and tack nails or screws.

7 Check again for square. If possible temporarily place the closet doors into the opening to be sure they and their hardware will fit with consistent gaps all around. Finish driving the nails or screws. Cut and install casing inside the closet.

INSTALLING BYPASS DOORS

A popular choice for closets, bypass doors need no room to swing open, but they allow access to only one side of a closet at a time. Hardware kits are available for openings of 4, 5, 6, and 8 feet. To accommodate a different opening width, simply cut a standard track with a hacksaw.

The kits are designed to work with standard 1⅜-inch-thick interior doors. If you use thicker doors, they may interfere with each other as they slide. Thinner doors may have a wide gap between them. The combined width of the doors should equal the width of the opening plus at least 1 inch. This provides ½ inch of overlap between the two doors when they are closed.

Some minor variations exist among bypass door kits from different manufacturers, but they are all easy to install. Check the manufacturer's directions carefully before you start.

PRESTART CHECKLIST

☐ **TIME**
About 1 hour for a pair of doors

☐ **TOOLS**
Drill/driver, level, tape measure

☐ **SKILLS**
Leveling the track, locating and installing hardware

☐ **PREP**
Finish the opening with wood jambs or drywall; casings can be installed later.

☐ **MATERIALS**
Bypass door hardware kit, doors, shims

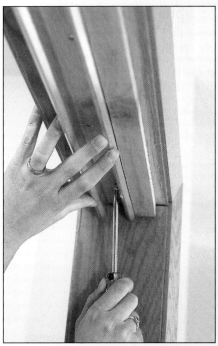

1 The position of the track depends on how you plan to trim the opening. Consult the manufacturer's instructions. Screw the track to the top of the door opening. Check to make sure the track is level; shim if necessary.

2 Attach the hangers to the tops of the doors. The hardware kit specifies exact locations. Tip the doors to hook the hangers onto the track. After the doors are hanging, install the center guide on the floor to keep the doors in line.

TRIM THE OPENING

Bare track installed for 1⅜-inch doors in drywall opening

Track installed in drywall opening hidden with casing

Track installed in opening with regular jamb and casing

When hanging bypass doors you have some options for finishing the opening. For utility applications simply hang the doors as is (left). For a more finished look, add trim to one (middle) or both sides of the header (right).

INSTALLING BIFOLD DOORS

Bifold doors can be installed easily in almost any opening. They can be used for closet doors, privacy, or controlling heat and airflow between rooms. Their advantages include ease of installation and minimal swing requirements. However, they take up more space in the door opening than swinging doors.

Bifold door kits—with plastic, metal, or wooden doors—come in a variety of styles, including louvered, paneled, and smooth. The kits fit most standard-width openings, although the maximum width of a single door is 24 inches. Units can be combined to cover openings up to 16 feet wide. Wooden doors can be trimmed for a better fit; plastic doors cannot be trimmed. (If you trim a wooden door kit, each door must be trimmed equally.) Two heights are available—one to fit standard 6-foot 8-inch openings, the other for 8-foot floor-to-ceiling applications. (See pages 134–135 for an overview of a bifold door installation.)

PRESTART CHECKLIST

☐ **TIME**
About 1 hour for a pair of doors

☐ **TOOLS**
Drill/driver, level, tape measure

☐ **SKILLS**
Leveling the track, locating and installing hardware

☐ **PREP**
The opening should be complete, with wooden jambs or drywall hung and finished; casings can be installed later.

☐ **MATERIALS**
Bifold door hardware kit, doors, shims

1 Bifold doors require a track similar to that used by bypass doors. Screw the track to the top of the opening. The doors pivot on pins protruding from the top and bottom. The pins engage brackets attached to the floor or jamb and the track.

2 Attach the roller or pin guide to the free end of the doors. This guide rides in the track and keeps the door in alignment.

BIFOLD DOOR TRIM OPTIONS

As with bypass doors you have trim options when installing a bifold door, depending on the look you are after.

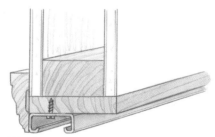

Wood header, flush mount

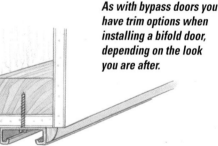

Drywall or plaster header, center mount, trimmed

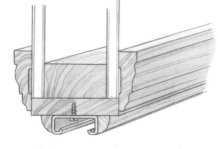

Wood header, center mount, trimmed

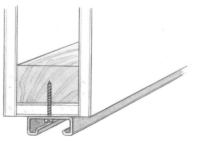

Drywall or plaster header, center mount

INSTALLING A POCKET DOOR

Install a single pocket door to save floor space—the door disappears into the wall when opened. While basic types are used for closets and bathrooms, heavier, more elaborate double pocket doors are available for areas where appearance is important.

There must be room for the pocket door to travel inside the wall. The wall must be wide enough for the door and it must be free of plumbing, wiring, or ductwork.

The pocket door frame shown here is available at many home centers and comes as a unit with the track already attached, making it easy to install. In some cases you may need to buy separate parts—including individual split jambs, spacers for the jambs, wheel carriers, and the overhead track—and install them one at a time.

Purchase the door and its hardware along with the frame, and make sure all the parts will be compatible. The door size must match the size of the pocket frame.

PRESTART CHECKLIST

☐ **TIME**
Once the rough opening is done, half a day to install the pocket door frame, the drywall, and the door; a day or two more to finish the wall

☐ **TOOLS**
Tape measure, hammer, level, drill, circular saw, drywall saw, screwdriver, nail set, tablesaw

☐ **SKILLS**
General carpentry, wall finishing

☐ **PREP**
Make sure there is room for the pocket door to slide into the wall, and cover the floor with a drop cloth.

☐ **MATERIALS**
Pocket door frame, pocket door with handle and wheel carriers, finishing nails or trimhead screws, jamb stock

1 Following manufacturer's specs, prepare an opening wide enough for the door frame. If there is an existing door, remove it and its jambs. Remove studs as needed (temporarily support the ceiling if the wall is load bearing—see pages 90–91) and install framing, including a header. Check the sides for plumb.

Header

2 The pocket door frame must be assembled. Position the header on top, seated in its groove, and drive finishing nails or screws to attach it to the split jambs.

POCKET DOOR INSTALLATION

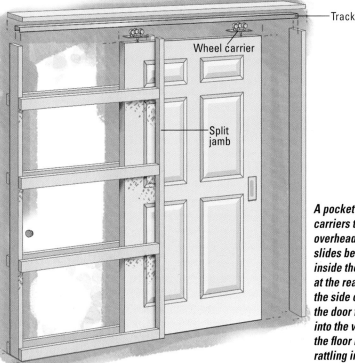

Track

Wheel carrier

Split jamb

A pocket door hangs on carriers that travel on an overhead track. The door slides between split jambs inside the wall. A bumper at the rear of the frame or the side of the door keeps the door from sliding too far into the wall, and guides at the floor keep the door from rattling inside the frame.

3 Attach the door frame to a stud and to the header. Use shims and check that the frame is kept square, level, and plumb. Attach the bumper to the rear of the frame (unless it will be attached to the door). If you are installing a set of two doors, install another frame on the other side.

4 Apply drywall to the frame using 1-inch drywall screws. Cut the drywall flush against the edges of the split jambs.

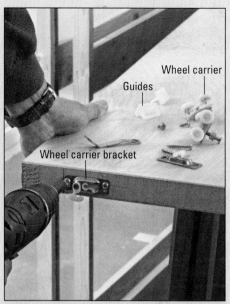

Guides
Wheel carrier
Wheel carrier bracket

5 Attach the wheel carrier bracket to the top of the door, several inches from each end. Slip the wheel carriers into the track. Attach the handles (these often need to be bought separately); you may need to bore holes first.

Locking device

6 Lift the door up and slip each wheel bracket onto its wheel carrier. (This can be difficult; you may have to adjust the wheel carrier mechanism so it is fully extended.) Close the locking device on each bracket. Check that the door glides smoothly.

Jamb, rip-cut to size

7 Rip a piece of jamb stock or 1× lumber to fit opposite the split jambs. The jambs should be flush with the surface of the drywall (usually ½-inch proud of the studs and the header). Attach the jambs with finishing nails or trimhead screws.

8 Cover the split jamb with trim. Cut and install casing (see pages 166–167). Install the guides provided with the door. Test the operation of the door.

INSTALLING DOOR AND WINDOW CASING

Casing is the molding that frames a door or window opening. In addition to dressing up the opening, casings cover the gaps between the walls and the jambs and hide the raw edge of the drywall. Before wrapping casing around a window or exterior door, add insulation. Loosely fill the gaps with shreds of fiberglass insulation poked in place with a drywall knife or similar tool or use nonexpanding spray foam insulation (page 175).

Casings usually are the same throughout a room, if not throughout a house, but that isn't a hard and fast rule. In fact, creating a hierarchy of casing details adds visual interest and richness to a room or home. Consider making the casings for exterior doors wider than those for interior doors and windows. Or adapt the casing size to suit the size of the opening: Larger openings get larger casings. Use your imagination.

PRESTART CHECKLIST

☐ **TIME**
About 45 minutes to an hour per door

☐ **TOOLS**
Tape measure, miter box and backsaw or mitersaw, hammer, nail set, drill/driver

☐ **SKILLS**
Measuring and laying out, cutting accurate miters, nailing, driving screws

☐ **PREP**
Walls should be finished (and painted, if possible) and door should be hung.

☐ **MATERIALS**
Molding; 4d, 6d, or 8d finishing nails (depending on molding thickness); 2-inch trimhead screws

1 Casings are usually positioned to leave ⅛ inch of the jamb's edge visible. This is called the reveal. To lay out the reveal, set a combination square to ⅛ inch or ¼ inch, hold a pencil in the notch on the edge, and draw a line along the head jamb and both side jambs.

2 Measure from the floor to the head casing reveal on both sides and cut side casings to length. Attach the side casings with five pairs of nails from top to bottom. Allow the nails to protrude in case you have to pull them to trim the casing or adjust its position when you fit the head casing.

DESIGN OPTION
Cutting butt joints

If your casings are flat boards, it's traditional—and easier—to use butt joints (top photo). In a butt joint the ends are cut square and the pieces butt together. Most often the head casing sits on top of the side casings, but occasionally the head casing is fitted between the side casings—it's a matter of preference.

Corner blocks (bottom photo) came into use during the Victorian era. They add a decorative element and allow butt joints to be used with ornate molded casings, which otherwise would have to be miter-cut. The blocks are slightly wider and thicker than the casing, making them the most forgiving way to wrap trim around a window or door opening.

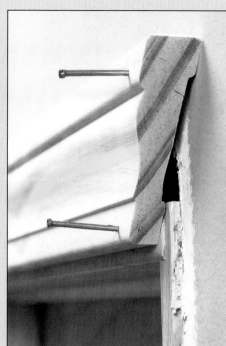

3 Most casings are backcut; that is, they have a shallow channel (or channels) cut in their backs. These channels allow for irregularities in the wall so the molding can fit tightly against the wall and jamb. When you install casing drive the nails through the solid edges.

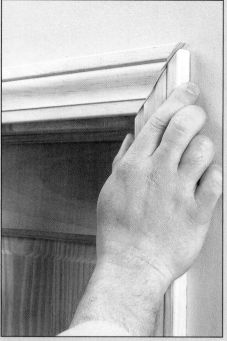

4 Cut the head casing roughly to length. If the molding is mitered as shown here, start with a piece that's a bit longer than needed and carefully trim it to fit. For butt-joined head casing (see opposite page), cut one end square and hold it in place to mark for an exact cut on the other side.

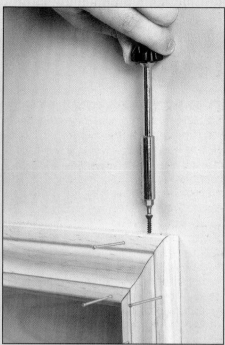

5 Nail the head casing to the wall and head jamb with three pairs of nails. As insurance against the miters opening, drill holes in the casing and drive 2-inch trimhead screws through the head casing into the side casings as shown. Set all the nailheads when you are happy with the fit.

Casing a window

Casing a window is just like casing a door, except the casings don't run all the way to the floor. Choose from two options: The traditional style has a sill that protrudes slightly into the room at the bottom of the window. The sill, which is technically called a stool, is the first piece of trim installed. The side casings then butt to the top of the sill. A piece of casing called an apron is applied under the sill as a finishing touch.

In less traditional construction the sill is eliminated and the casing is wrapped around the window like a picture frame (page 103). This technique demands a little more joint-making skill. No clear starting point exists; just pick one of the sides and go from there.

1 Traditional window trim begins with the stool. Use a jigsaw (page 101) to cut the horns on either end so they fit tightly against the drywall and the sides of the jambs.

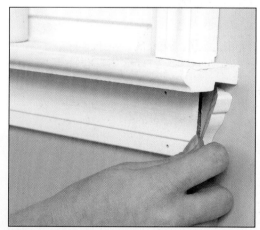

2 The apron is attached under the stool as the final piece of window trim. Measure between the outsides of the side casings to determine the apron length. If the apron has a molded profile, miter the ends of the apron toward the wall. Then glue a tiny piece of molding as a return to the wall (page 101).

FRAMING FOR A NEW EXTERIOR DOOR

Once you've determined the location for a new entry door, check for obstacles in the wall. Often a quick look from the basement or crawlspace will tell you what's hidden inside the wall above. But expect the unexpected when cutting into a wall and work carefully to avoid damaging utility lines.

Water pipes or electrical cables can often be moved without a great deal of difficulty, but check with a plumber or electrician first. Drainpipes and heating or air-conditioning ducts are difficult to move; if one is in the way, you may have to relocate the doorway.

Also determine what sort of stairway you will need outside. By looking at an existing door's bottom in relation to the house's siding, you can tell how high the stairway will need to be. Consult manufacturer's instructions for the correct width and height of the rough opening you will frame. The method shown here minimizes drywall work.

PRESTART CHECKLIST

☐ **TIME**
Most of a day to cut a drywall opening, make a frame for a door, and cut the siding

☐ **TOOLS**
Tape measure, stud finder, drill, flat pry bar, hand drywall saw, circular saw, reciprocating saw, level, framing square

☐ **SKILLS**
Removing wall materials, cutting lumber and building wall framing

☐ **PREP**
Determine that no electrical, plumbing, or duct lines are in the way, or plan to move the lines.

☐ **MATERIALS**
Framing lumber (either 2×4 or 2×6), header lumber (2×6 or larger, plus ½-inch plywood), 3-inch screws, 16d and 12d nails

1 Use a stud finder to determine the locations of your studs and plan the opening. Use a level to draw lines for the final rough opening and check for square, plumb, and level. Draw lines 1½ inches outside these from floor to ceiling. Cut out and remove the drywall (see page 28).

2 Use a circular saw, then a reciprocating saw, to cut through each exposed stud in two places. If you are confident of your measuring and cutting skills, you can cut the bottom of these studs to serve as the bottom of the cripples (see below and step 13), but they must be cut straight and square.

EXTERIOR DOOR FRAMING

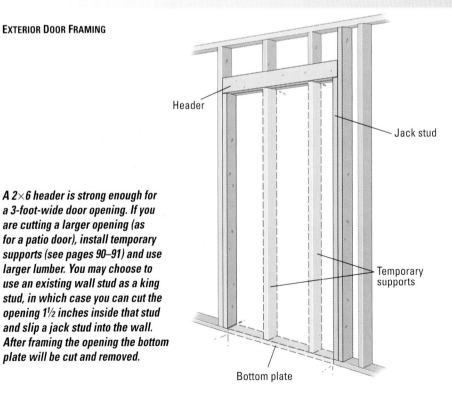

A 2×6 header is strong enough for a 3-foot-wide door opening. If you are cutting a larger opening (as for a patio door), install temporary supports (see pages 90–91) and use larger lumber. You may choose to use an existing wall stud as a king stud, in which case you can cut the opening 1½ inches inside that stud and slip a jack stud into the wall. After framing the opening the bottom plate will be cut and removed.

Header

Jack stud

Temporary supports

Bottom plate

3 Pry away the studs and pull them off the bottom plate. For safety while you work, pound exposed nails out of the exterior wall or bend them.

4 Mark the locations of king and jack studs. Studs are 1½ inches thick. Check that the distance between the jack studs equals the width of the rough opening.

5 Assemble a king-and-jack-stud combination. Cut the jack stud to the height of the rough opening, minus 1½ inches (to allow for the thickness of the bottom plate). Cut the king stud to reach from the bottom plate to the top plate. Place the jack stud on top of the king stud and nail or screw the pieces together.

6 Tap the king-and-jack combination into position and use a level to check that it is plumb. Place the jack stud about ¼ inch inside the layout line (it will move over when you drive the fastener).

7 Angle-drive nails or screws to attach the studs to the bottom plate. Also angle-drive fasteners down through the faces of the studs. Attach them to the top plate the same way.

8 If you will use an existing stud as a king stud, cut a jack stud and attach it to the existing stud. Carefully align the front edge of the jack stud with the front edge of the existing stud.

9 To construct a header, cut two (three with 2×6 framing as shown) pieces of 2×6 (or larger) to the width of the rough opening, plus 3 inches (to allow for the thickness of the two jack studs). Cut ½-inch plywood spacers. Working on the floor, stack the pieces with the crowns facing the same direction (see next step) and use a square to make sure they are aligned. Fasten the pieces by driving two 3-inch screws or 16d nails every 8 inches or so.

10 Sight along the header to determine its crown, where it bulges upward in the middle. Place the header, crown side up, on top of the jack studs. You may need to tap the header into place.

13 Cut short cripple studs to fit between the header and the top plate. Tap them in where the old studs used to be. Drill pilot holes (short pieces like this are prone to splitting) and attach with angle-driven screws or nails.

14 Use a reciprocating saw to cut the bottom plate straight down to the floor. Pry the plate out.

15 Drill 1-inch holes through the siding at each corner. Slip a reciprocating saw blade into a hole and cut through the siding, using the jack studs and header as guides. (If you have stucco siding, first cut away the stucco; see page 30.)

11 Attach the header with angle-driven screws or nails. If you have removed a wide section of drywall, you can instead drive fasteners through the outside face of the king studs.

12 Check that the opening is square, level, and plumb. It need not be perfect, but it should be pretty close. If you have doubts set the door temporarily in place to make sure it will fit. If the opening is not square, you may be able to remove fasteners at the top and move the king studs over.

16 Have a helper or two catch the siding and sheathing section as it falls. Cut the section into disposable pieces and cart it away to the trash.

WHAT IF...
You're working with balloon framing?

Most homes have platform framing, with studs that span between a bottom and top plate. Some older homes have balloon framing, in which the studs travel up through the floor and the ceiling, with no plates. If you have balloon framing, you will need to cut the studs to the height of the floor joists (that is, the bottom of the subflooring). Also cut and install short cripple studs for each side and cut a piece of subflooring to fit.

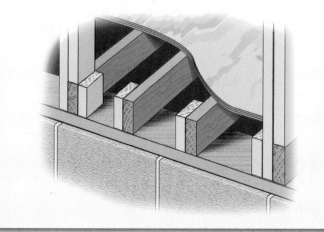

INSTALLING A PREHUNG EXTERIOR DOOR

An exterior door is heavy, so have it delivered unless you have a truck, and enlist one or two assistants to help you move it into place.

See pages 18–23 for types and styles of doors to consider. You may need to wait a week or two for delivery of the door that's just right for you. Measure the width of an existing doorjamb or measure the thickness of your rough opening to be sure the jamb is the correct width for your wall; the front interior jamb edges should be flush with your drywall or plaster.

Many prehungs come with brick molding for the exterior, but you may choose to install your own moldings (see pages 142–143).

Start with a rough opening that is correctly sized and reasonably square, level, and plumb (see pages 168–171).

PRESTART CHECKLIST

☐ **TIME**
About 4 hours to install a door with standard trim inside and out

☐ **TOOLS**
Tape measure, drill, hammer, level, tin snips, chisel, circular saw, stapler, caulk gun, screwdriver, nail set, reciprocating saw, utility knife

☐ **SKILLS**
Basic finish carpentry skills

☐ **PREP**
Frame the rough opening or remove an existing door and prepare the rough opening.

☐ **MATERIALS**
Prehung exterior door, metal drip edge, exterior brick molding, interior casing, casing nails, finishing nails, composite shims, exterior caulk, wood filler, fiberglass or foam insulation

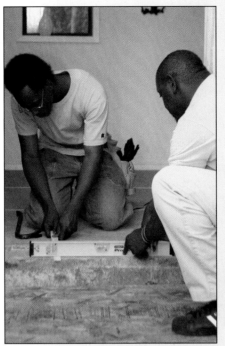

1 Check the floor for level and shim if needed. Place a pair of shims—one facing each way, so the surface will be level—every 8 inches or so and nail them in place.

2 Uncrate the door (see below) and set it in the opening. Check for level and plumb, and shim as needed. Tack (partially drive) nails or screws to hold it in place temporarily.

STANLEY PRO TIP: **Preparing the door**

Place the door on a smooth surface and remove the hinge and corner guards. If there are plastic inserts or blocks holding the door closed, do not remove them until you set the door in the opening.

If a prehung is out of square—that is, if the gap between the door and the jamb is wider on one side—you can usually straighten it. Tilt it so it rests on one bottom corner and pull down as needed.

3 Check that the door operates smoothly and that the gap between the door and the jambs is consistent all around. To be sure, you may want to install the lockset at this time (see pages 138–141).

4 Mark around the door's brick molding for cutting the siding (see page 29). Or hold the molding you will use in place and mark. Use a handsaw to finish the cuts at the bottom if a circular saw can't complete the cut. Use a chisel at the corners.

5 Slightly pry away the siding all around and use a reciprocating saw to cut through any nails within 6 inches of the opening. Slip in strips of roofing felt or building paper, wrap them around the framing, and attach with staples.

STANLEY. PRO TIP

Drip cap arrangement

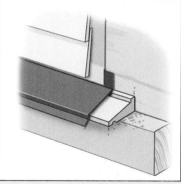

Some prehung doors come with a plastic or wood drip cap at the top that is sloped to allow water to flow easily away from the house. If your unit does not have a drip cap, install one. The drip edge flashing fits over the drip cap and slips under the roofing felt or building paper.

6 Cut a piece of metal drip edge flashing and slip it up behind the roofing felt. Use a scrap of trim to confirm that you've allowed enough space. The drip edge should incline slightly to direct water away from the house.

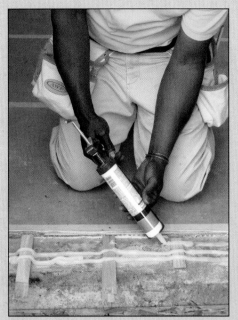

7 Apply three beads of caulk at the sill plate before you set the door into place. If you have installed shims, apply extra-thick beads to ensure that the threshold will be sealed at all points.

8 With a helper lift the door's threshold onto the caulk (avoid sliding, which would weaken the caulk seal) and tilt the door into the opening. Make sure the brick molding seats against the sheathing.

9 Tap in shims as needed all around and check the sides for plumb. Also check that the door operates smoothly and there is a consistent gap between door and jambs all around.

STANLEY PRO TIP

Dealing with an out-of-square opening

If a prehung door is not square, level, and operating smoothly—because the rough opening is not square or plumb—don't settle for a less-than-perfect arrangement; the door will never work well. Remove the door and fix the opening. If a stud needs to move over only a bit, you may be able to persuade it with a small sledgehammer. Otherwise remove fasteners at the bottom or top of both studs, move them over, and reattach.

13 Attach the threshold by driving screws into the sheathing. Wipe away any caulking that oozes out. If the threshold has a rubber gasket, install it.

14 Drive casing nails to attach the brick molding. Use a nail set to drive the heads slightly below the wood surface. Fill the holes with wood filler and sand smooth.

10 Attach the hinge-side jamb first, using 10d casing nails. If possible, drive the nails where they will be covered with stop molding. Drive nails near the shims and check that the jamb has not become bent.

11 Nail the latch side in the same way, constantly checking for a consistent gap between door and jamb—a piece of cardboard from a note pad makes a good gauge. Nail the header jamb as well.

12 At each hinge remove two screws and drive in 3-inch screws with the same size heads. These screws add considerable strength and stability to a door.

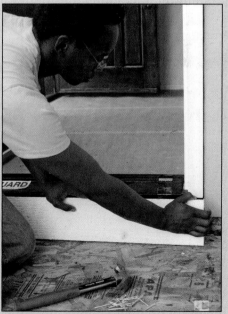

15 Cut the shims inside. You can often score them with a utility knife and break them off. Or cut them with a handsaw (page 99). Cut them flush with the jamb edges, but take care not to mar the jambs.

16 Spray nonexpanding foam or gently insert pieces of fiberglass insulation between the jambs and the framing (see page 99).

17 If siding is exposed below the door, it will be vulnerable to damage by foot traffic. Cut out and replace the siding with a 1× kick board or install the kick board over the siding.

INSTALLING A STORM DOOR

A high-quality storm door correctly installed provides a good measure of protection against the weather. If you also apply weatherstripping (pages 144–145), you'll have a doorway that is nearly as well insulated as the surrounding wall. In addition, a storm door prolongs the life of the entry door by protecting it from the elements.

Many storm doors are flimsy affairs made of single-thickness aluminum, with poor weatherstripping and hinges that are likely to come loose. You'll save money in the long run if you buy a quality unit. Look for substantial weatherstripping around the glass panes and the door itself. The frame and hinge should be sturdy enough to stand up to wind gusts. The door frame should be insulated or made of clad wood. The door bottom should have a thick rubber seal that can be adjusted and, when necessary, replaced.

Inspect the opening where the storm door will be installed. The frame and molding should be fairly square and reasonably smooth, so the storm door can seal well. At the bottom the sill or threshold should be an even plane so the door's sweep can seal at all points (see step 7).

PRESTART CHECKLIST

☐ **TIME**
About 3 hours to install a storm door

☐ **TOOLS**
Tape measure, drill, hammer, level, tin snips, hacksaw, pliers, framing square, caulk gun, screwdriver, nail set

☐ **SKILLS**
Measuring, leveling, fastening

☐ **PREP**
Measure the opening and purchase a storm door to fit.

☐ **MATERIALS**
Storm door with latch and other hardware, caulk

1 Uncrate the door and remove screen panes as recommended by the manufacturer. Position the metal drip cap against the brick molding at the top and temporarily install it with one screw only. (These steps may not apply to all doors; follow the manufacturer's instructions.)

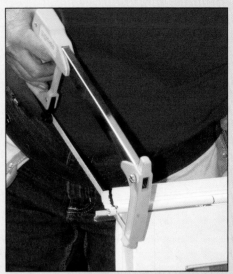

2 Measure the distance from the underside of the drip cap to the sill. Determine which end of the hinge-side Z bar is up. Measure and cut the bottom of the Z bar. If the sill is sloped, make an angled cut that follows the slope.

MEASURING AND INSTALLING A STORM DOOR

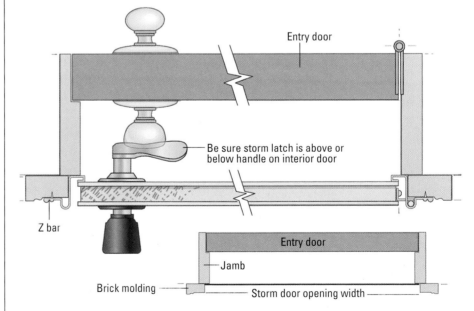

Entry door

Be sure storm latch is above or below handle on interior door

Z bar

Entry door

Jamb

Brick molding

Storm door opening width

A storm door typically attaches to the exterior molding. To order a door to fit, measure the opening between the side moldings and from the sill to the underside of the top molding. If you have a doorway that is taller than 80 inches, you may need to order a custom-size door. When installing the storm door handle, make sure it will not bump into the entry door handle.

3 Set the door in the opening, with the top of the Z bar butted against the end of the drip cap. If needed, adjust the position of the drip cap or trim the bottom of the Z bar. Temporarily fasten the door with screws at the top and the bottom.

4 Check for plumb. Test that the door operates smoothly. Adjust as necessary and finish fastening the Z bar. Close the door. Adjust the drip cap so there is a consistent gap of 1/8 inch between it and the door. Drive screws through the remaining holes to attach the drip cap.

5 Measure and cut the latch-side Z bar. Hold it up against the end of the drip cap and drive two screws to hold it in place. Test the fit of the door and adjust the Z bar's position as needed to achieve a consistent 1/8-inch gap. Drive the rest of the screws.

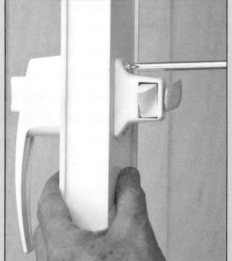

6 Close the door and check that it seals snugly against the weatherstripping at all points. If needed, adjust the positions of the Z bar or the drip cap. Insert the handle parts from each side and drive screws to attach the parts. Attach the latch and adjust so the door closes tightly.

7 Slip the sweep onto the bottom of the door, close the door, and adjust so the sweep's fins touch the sill and compress slightly. Drive screws to secure the sweep.

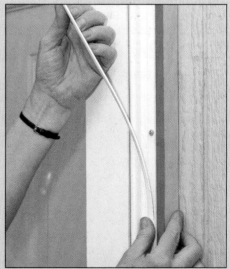

8 Install the closer and perhaps a wind chain (see page 132). Some doors come with a cover that fits in a channel to hide the screws. Cut it to length and snap it in place.

INSTALLING A PATIO DOOR

A sliding or swinging patio door installs using many of the same steps as for a standard entry door (pages 172–175). However, because it is so large, requirements are more exacting. The frame must be straight and square all along its length; it is particularly important that the sill be straight and level.

Some patio doors are sold with the frame knocked down, so you will need to assemble it. It may be easier to purchase a door with the frame already assembled.

The steps that follow show a sliding patio door. For installing a pair of hinged (French) patio doors, see page 183.

If you are replacing a patio door that operates smoothly, you may not need to alter the rough opening. However, if the old door was difficult to operate, check the rough opening carefully.

PRESTART CHECKLIST

☐ **TIME**
After the rough opening is prepared, about 4 hours

☐ **TOOLS**
Tape measure, drill, hammer, level, tin snips, chisel, circular saw, flat pry bar, stapler, caulk gun, screwdriver, nail set, handsaw

☐ **SKILLS**
Measuring, sawing, fastening, leveling

☐ **PREP**
Assemble the door frame if needed. Enlist a helper.

☐ **MATERIALS**
Patio door, metal drip edge, roofing felt or building paper, mason's line, exterior brick molding, interior casing, casing nails, finishing nails, composite shims, exterior caulk, wood filler, insulation

1 Remove the old patio door. (To cut and frame a new opening, see pages 168–171. If you make a new opening, install a temporary support—see pages 90–91.) Measure the diagonals to check the opening for square (they should be exactly equal). Use a long straight board or a string line to check for high spots in the sill and low spots on the header. When measuring for a new door, use the shortest measurements. Use shims to level the sill (page 172).

SEALING A PATIO DOOR

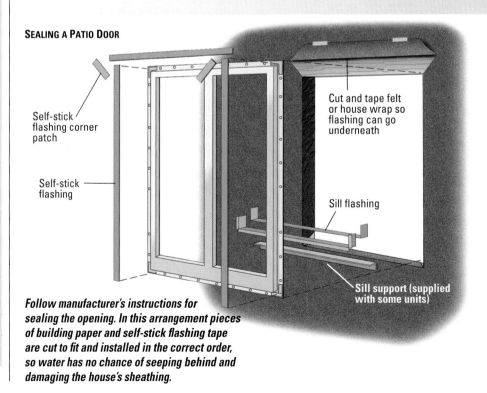

Self-stick flashing corner patch

Self-stick flashing

Cut and tape felt or house wrap so flashing can go underneath

Sill flashing

Sill support (supplied with some units)

Follow manufacturer's instructions for sealing the opening. In this arrangement pieces of building paper and self-stick flashing tape are cut to fit and installed in the correct order, so water has no chance of seeping behind and damaging the house's sheathing.

2 On a wide opening like this, also check that the sides are in the same plane. If one side leans away from the house and the other does not, the opening is "cross-legged" and the door will not slide smoothly. Stretch two lines diagonally across the opening; they should just touch where they cross. If they don't, try using a small sledgehammer to move one or both sides a bit. Otherwise you may need to remove siding or drywall on one side and adjust the framing.

3 Prepare the sill according to manufacturer's instructions. In this arrangement self-adhesive flashing is applied along the sill. See pages 84–85 and 173 for more instructions.

4 Unpack the door and assemble as necessary. If the sliding panel is in place, remove it by lifting up and tilting the bottom out. It's usually best to leave the fixed panel in place; it makes the door heavy, but it helps keep the frame square. Some packing blocks should be removed; others should be left in place until you're ready to install the molding. Refer to the manufacturer's instructions.

Countersink bit

5 The door shown is held in place with fasteners driven through the jamb. For a neat installation use a countersink bit to drill holes so the screw heads will be flush with the surface. Locate the holes according to the manufacturer's instructions. (For installing a unit with flanges, see pages 104–105.)

6 Working with at least one helper, lift the door onto the sill and tilt it in. Press the unit into position against the siding. Have a helper hold the door in place while you make adjustments.

7 Check the door frame for level, square, and plumb; continually recheck as you shim. Tap in pairs of shims every 12 inches on the sides and the header, and every 8 inches on the floor. Tack (partially drive) nails or screws to temporarily hold the door in place. Reinstall the sliding panel and check for smooth operation. If your patio door has brick molding already attached, mark the siding (page 104) for cutting now. See pages 29 and 83 for cutting methods. Back out the fasteners and remove the door.

10 Install the sliding door and test for smooth operation. The gap between the door panel and the frame should be consistent at all points. Drive screws or nails to attach the threshold. If you see the threshold flex slightly when you slide the door, install additional shims as needed.

11 Drive nails or screws to attach the side jambs. At the strike (or strike box), install shims and drive a long screw to secure the strike. Install the latch, test, and adjust as needed.

8 Just before you finally install the door, apply three beads of exterior caulk on the sill. Apply extra-thick caulk near shims to be sure the bottom of the threshold seals against the sill. Tilt the door back in place. Check that the threshold is straight and even. Shim the sides and the header.

9 If the door's jambs are the right width, the front of the jambs will be flush with the wall surface. Often, however, the jambs fall short of the wall surface. If so, make sure the distance between the jamb face and the wall surface is consistent all around, so you can fill in later with trim ripped to fit. If the jamb stands slightly proud of the wall surface, you will need to plane the jamb.

12 Drive screws to install the head jamb. Slide the door and check the gap for consistency. You may need to back out some screws, adjust the shims, and redrive the screws.

13 Use a handsaw to cut the shims flush with the framing or the wall surface. If the jamb does not come flush with the wall surface, cut the shims flush with the jamb edges. If the sill does not stick out as far as the brick molding, rip-cut a piece of siding or pressure-treated lumber to fit and nail or screw it in place. You can install a kick board below the sill (page 175).

14 Mark a ¼-inch reveal around the exterior edge of the jamb (page 100). Hold trim against the door for marking. Apply the trim using 10d galvanized casing nails when nailing into framing and 6d if nailing into the jamb. Use 10d galvanized casing nails for attaching integral brick molding. For flanged units drive screws.

15 Rip-cut the jamb extender (see step 9 on page 180 for how to measure for the extender). To ease final installation, glue the extenders to the interior casing in advance. (In this case the old casing could be reused because the replacement door was slightly smaller than the original door.) Be sure to clamp each piece even with the casing.

WHAT IF…
You are installing a French patio door?

A set of hinged patio doors installs much like a slider but also has some of the challenges of hanging a standard exterior door (pages 172–175). Because two doors meet in the middle, any sagging or out-of-square condition will be multiplied. Provide extra strength for the hinges by removing one hinge screw and driving a 3-inch screw through the hole into the wall framing.

When shimming and aligning the unit, pay special attention to the critical point where the two doors meet. The doors should fit snugly but not so tightly that they are difficult to operate. (On wood units there is often a special piece of molding called a T astragal on the vertical edge of one of the doors.)

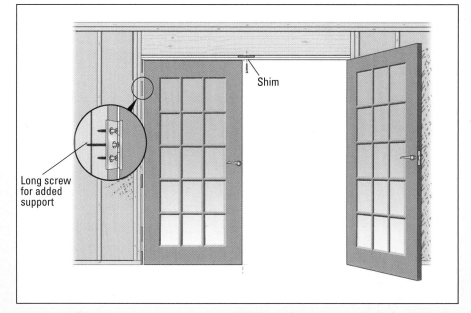

Shim

Long screw for added support

16 With the rip-cut pieces of 1× glued to the casing, it can be trimmed to fit and reattached to the wall. For more on cutting and installing interior casing, see pages 166–167.

17 The sliding panel can be adjusted up or down on one or both sides by turning an adjusting screw. The screw may be on the bottom face of the panel or at either end.

18 Check the screen panel for square. If it is out of square, stand it on one corner and pull down on the opposite corner. Install the sliding screen and adjust it so it slides easily.

19 Apply a bead of exterior caulk all around the exterior trim. Set any nails below the surface. Fill nail or screw holes with a dot of caulk.

GARAGE DOOR MAINTENANCE AND WEATHERSTRIPPING

A garage door is a large, heavy moving part that endures repeated use and exposure to the weather. Over time this stress causes fasteners to loosen and fall out of alignment, with the result that the garage door becomes difficult to open. Regular maintenance is the best way to keep a garage door in smooth working order.

A few times a year, check for loose parts and oil the moving parts. A little oil keeps moving parts from rusting and ensures they will do their job quietly and smoothly.

THREE TYPES OF GARAGE DOOR

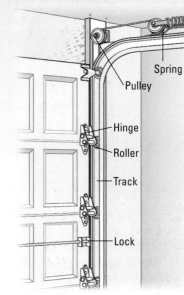

The most common type of garage door is the sectional roll-up door. It has four or more horizontal sections connected with hinges and rolls on tracks located on both sides of the door. The door first opens up, then back.

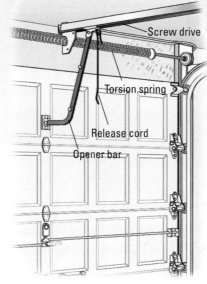

Newer roll-up doors have a single torsion spring running across the header. A motor pulls the door up via a long screw drive bolted to the center of the ceiling.

An older tilt-up (or swing-up) garage door is made of a single large panel that pivots out and up. On each side two hinge arms guide the movement, and a spring keeps the door open or closed.

SAFETY FIRST
Call a pro for spring repairs

A door that seems unusually heavy to lift may need its springs serviced. Garage door springs are under extreme tension because of the heavy load they lift. **It is dangerous for a homeowner to attempt to replace or adjust the springs; the heavy door and the spring under tension both pose hazards.** To be safe call a garage door professional. Likewise, never remove a cable while the door spring is under tension. If released it can lash out and cause injury.

Track alignment

Misaligned tracks make the door difficult to open. First see that the tracks are solidly bolted at the wall and ceiling. Then check for alignment. To adjust, loosen the track's mounting bolt and use a hammer and a wood block to slide it back into position, then retighten the bolt.

Electric opener

Sometimes a malfunctioning electric opener can cause garage door balkiness. To check for this possibility, disconnect the opener by pulling the release cord. Open the door manually. If it works, the problem is with the opener. Consult the owner's manual.

Garage door tune-up

1 Close the door and disconnect the garage door opener, if you have one. Or slide the locking bar into the track to keep the door from opening while you work. Look for loose or missing nuts or bolts. Steel doors usually have lag screws holding hinges in place, while wood doors have bolts that go all the way through the door, with nuts on the hinge side. Replace and tighten as needed.

2 Wipe along the inside of the track using a cloth dampened with a solution of dish soap and water to remove any oil or accumulated dirt. Avoid lubricating the track; the oil can attract debris. Spray lubricant onto the garage door's hinges. Also squirt a few drops of oil on the roller bearings of each wheel so they will spin quietly and easily in the tracks. Wipe off any excess.

3 Coat the springs with a generous spray of lubricant to promote smooth operation and rust resistance. Don't wipe off any excess. Lubricate the garage door opener chain or screw drive by spraying on white lithium grease, available at hardware or auto stores or at home centers. This will help minimize stress on the opener's motor.

Hinges and rollers

Look for cracks or chips in nylon rollers and for wear to steel bearings or wheels. If a wheel tilts replace it. Remove a damaged wheel by loosening the lag screws or nuts on the hinges. **Do not remove the bottom hinge or roller: The cable attached to it is under extreme tension.** Tilt the hinge away from the door and slip the wheel out of its rail. Slip the shaft of the new wheel into the hinge and tip it into the rail. Retighten the lag screws or nuts.

Replacing garage door weatherstripping

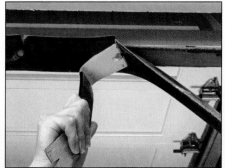

Remove any old weatherstripping, sand the edge surface, and apply a clear wood preservative. In most cases the weatherstrip should be attached with the overhang facing toward the inside. If it faces outside it may hit the garage door frame when the door opens and you may need to trim it. If the area just outside the door is significantly lower than the bottom edge of the door, you can install the weatherstripping with the overhang to face outside.

Put the door at a comfortable working height. Tack the weatherstrip in place with staples first, stapling every 3 inches or so. You'll attach the weatherstripping at the ends last. Then nail it on between the staples. If the nails that come with the weatherstripping are $1/2$ inch in length, discard them and use 1-inch-long galvanized roofing nails instead for better gripping power. Occasionally lubricate the weatherstripping to keep it supple.

GLOSSARY

Apron: The bottom piece of window casing that finishes the window frame beneath the interior sill. (See also Stool.)

Balloon framing: An older type of construction in which studs run continuously from floor to floor, with no top or bottom plates. (See also Plate).

Baseboard: Trim running along the bottom of a wall to cover gaps between the wall and floor.

Bearing wall: A wall that carries a portion of the weight of the building above it.

Bevel cut: A cut that runs at an angle through the thickness of a board or piece of trim.

Bifold door: A door, often used for a closet, that folds in half as it opens.

Bolt: The part of a door latch that slides horizontally and inserts into the strike when the door is closed.

Bow: A defect in which a board is warped along its length when viewed along its narrow dimension.

Brick molding: A type of exterior casing, usually thick and narrow, used not only for brick homes but also for homes with siding and often factory-applied to windows or prehung doors.

Butt joint: The joint formed by two pieces of material cut at 90 degrees when fastened end to end, end to face, or end to edge.

Bypass doors: Closet doors that open by sliding past each other.

Casing: Trim that lies flat surrounding a door or window opening to conceal the gap between jamb and wall.

Corner bead: A plastic or metal molding that is attached to outside drywall corners to make them easier to finish and to protect them from damage.

Countersink: To drive the head of a nail or screw so that its top is flush with the surface of the surrounding wood.

Cripple stud: A short stud, typically used above headers in door and window openings and below sill plates in window openings.

Crosscut: To cut a board to length, across the wood's grain.

Dead bolt: A locking device activated only with a key or thumb turn. Unlike the beveled tongue of a latch, a dead bolt has a squared-off end.

Drip edge: Metal or plastic flashing installed above a door or window, to ensure water will run away from the house.

Drywall: A sheet product made for use as a wall surface, consisting of paper faces covering a core of gypsum.

Flashing: A formed metal or plastic sheet, or a strip of flexible self-stick material, used to protect the house (or a window or door) from moisture and to direct water away.

Framing: The structure of the house, including all the wooden (or metal) parts of a house's frame—wall studs, headers, joists, rafters, etc. The term "frame" is sometimes also used to describe the jambs surrounding a window or door.

Header: The part of a house's frame that spans the top of a door or window opening, often made from two pieces of 2× lumber with a spacer of $1/2$-inch plywood.

House wrap: A fibrous sheeting applied on exterior wall sheathing. It helps limit air flow through walls, protects from wind-driven rain, and allows vapor to escape from within.

Jack stud: One part of the pairs of studs that frame a door or window opening. Jack studs, sometimes called trimmers, are cut to match the height of the opening. The header rests on top of the jack studs. (See also king stud.)

Jamb: The wooden frame, usually $3/4$-inch thick and as wide as the total thickness of the wall, that surrounds a window or door opening.

Jamb extension: Pieces of wood applied to the edge of a jamb to make it the same thickness as the wall.

Joist: A horizontal part of a house's frame that supports the floor and/or ceiling.

King stud: One part of the pairs of studs that frame a door or window opening. King studs are cut to the same length as other wall studs. Jack studs are nailed to the king studs.

Lath: Thin strips of wood applied to a wall surface to serve as a substrate for plaster. More recent plasterwork often uses metal mesh or pieces of gypsum board as lath.

Level: Perfectly horizontal with no part higher or lower than another. Also, a tool used to assess this condition.

Light (or lite): Glass sections in a window or door.

Load-bearing wall: Also called a bearing wall. A wall that carries a portion of the weight of the building above it.

Lockset: The hardware used for keeping a door closed, usually consisting of doorknobs, lock, bolt, and strike plate.

Low-E glass: A type of glass with a thin coating that reflects radiant heat and ultraviolet rays.

Miter: A corner joint between two pieces of wood where the adjoining ends are cut at matching angles (usually, two 45-degree angles that meet to form a 90-degree angle). Also, the process of cutting these angles.

Molding: Lumber or other material that has been milled to various decorative profiles. Molding (also called trim) is used to cover gaps between materials and to add visual interest.

Mortise: A shallow recess cut so that a piece of hardware, such as a hinge leaf or a strike plate, can fit and be flush with the surrounding wood surface.

Mullion: A narrow vertical piece that divides glass sections in a single window or door.

Muntin: A narrow piece of wood that divides glass openings in a window sash or a door with lights.

On-center (OC): A phrase used to designate the distance from the center of one regularly spaced framing member to the center of the next.

Parting stop: A narrow strip of wood that separates the sashes of a double-hung window.

Pilot hole: A hole bored prior to driving a screw or nail, to ensure against splitting the board. A pilot hole is slightly narrower than the fastener being driven through it.

Plate: A horizontal piece of lumber to which the wall studs are attached. The bottom plate is anchored to the floor. The top plate is usually double in thickness to tie walls together and to help carry the load from above.

Platform framing: The most common type of framing, in which studs span the height of one floor only, from bottom to top plate.

Plumb: Perfectly vertical. This can be determined using a level or a plumb bob.

Plywood: A sheet product made from thin layers of wood (veneers) glued in a sandwich. Generally available in 4×8-foot sheets.

Prehung door: A door that is purchased already hinged and hanging within a complete door jamb.

Rabbet: A groove cut across the width of a board at its end, into which a crosspiece is fit for a secure joint.

Rafters: Roof framing members installed parallel to each other and running from wall to ridge or wall to wall.

Rail: A horizontal piece on a panel door or a window sash.

Return: When used with regard to trim, a piece of molding that completes a run by turning into the wall.

Reveal: A narrow flat area on a molding or board (usually, a jamb edge) left uncovered for visual effect.

Rip: To cut a board along its length in order to trim it to the desired width.

Rough opening: The opening in the framing made to accommodate a door or window's jambs.

R-value: A way of measuring a material's resistance to heat transfer.

Sash: A frame containing a piece of glass.

Sash cord or chain: A rope or chain that connects a window sash to a weight or a spring. In an older window, the cord or chain connects to a weight that travels inside a cavity between the window jambs and the house framing.

Sheathing: A layer of sheet goods or (in older homes) planks that covers the studs and is covered by siding.

Shim: A wedge, usually made of wood or composite material, used to align jambs and other materials in a rough opening.

Sill: A trim piece at the bottom of a window or door, sloped so water can run away from the house. Or, the framing piece at the bottom of a door.

Snapping a line: A term used to describe the process of marking a layout line using a chalk line tool. Held taut between two points and plucked so it snaps against the surface, the chalk line transfers a straight line of chalk onto the surface.

Square: A 90-degree angle.

Stile: A vertical piece on a panel door or a window sash.

Stool: A horizontal piece of trim installed at the bottom of a window inside the house, often called the sill.

Stop: A narrow strip of wood installed inside a doorjamb that keeps the door from swinging too far when it closes.

Strike: The metal hardware attached to the doorjamb that receives the bolt from the lockset. Also called a strike plate.

Stucco: A finish composed of two or more layers of Portland cement, sand, and lime applied to the exterior of a structure.

Stud: A vertical member of a house's frame, often made from 2×4s or 2×6s.

Subfloor: The first layer of decking applied on top of the floor joists. Usually made from plywood, but in pre-WWII homes made from diagonally run planks.

Threshold: Also called a saddle, a wood or metal piece that lies on the floor at the bottom of a door and spans the flooring materials of the two adjacent rooms.

Toenailing: Driving a nail at an angle through one framing member so it can penetrate a second framing member.

U-value: The tendency to transfer heat. U-value is the inverse of R-value.

Warp: A surface that is not true or flat.

INDEX

KNOWLEDGE IS THE BEST TOOL

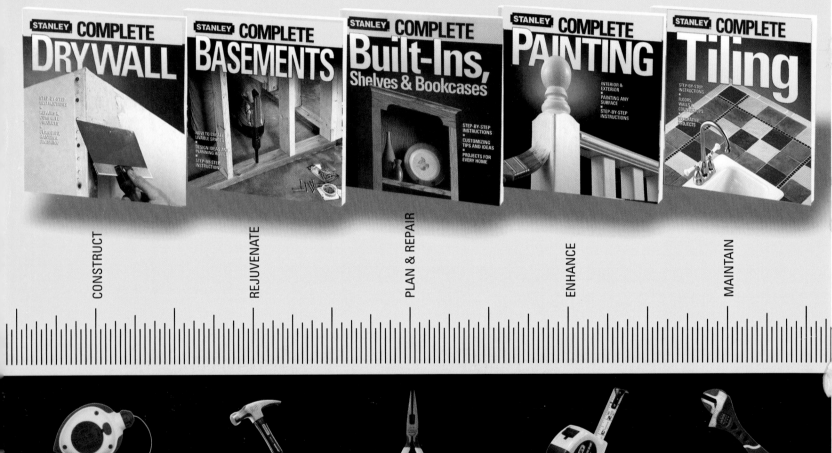

STANLEY COMPLETE **DRYWALL**

STANLEY COMPLETE **BASEMENTS**

STANLEY COMPLETE **Built-Ins,** Shelves & Bookcases

STANLEY COMPLETE **PAINTING**

STANLEY COMPLETE **Tiling**

CONSTRUCT

REJUVENATE

PLAN & REPAIR

ENHANCE

MAINTAIN